Quilts
for Guys

EDITED BY CYNDY LYLE RYMER

15 Fun Projects for
Your Favorite Fella

C&T PUBLISHING

To John, Kevin, Zack, and Zana, who understand when I have to sew. And to everyone at C&T, thanks for all of the great brainstorming and moral support. *Cyndy Lyle Rymer*

To Michael, Peder, and Beret, who understand how sewing feeds my soul. *Carolyn Aune*

To all of the quilters who helped make this book a reality: a heartfelt thank you! It was a pleasure working with all of you.

Many thanks to Classic Cottons and Cranston Print Works Company for their generous donations of novelty fabrics, and to all of the fabric manufacturers who continue to make those fun novelty prints.

Copyright © 2001 by C&T Publishing

Development Editor: Cyndy Lyle Rymer
Technical Editor: Carolyn Aune
Design Director: Aliza Kahn Shalit
Book and Cover Design: Aliza Kahn Shalit
Graphic Illustrations: Aliza Kahn Shalit, AK Design
Production Coordinator: Diane Pedersen
Production Assistant: Kirstie L. McCormick
Cover Images: Details from *Midnight Hoop Dreams* by Cyndy Rymer and *Little Guys Are Great* by Sandy Bonsib.

Attention Teachers:

C&T Publishing, Inc. encourages you to use this book as a text for teaching. Contact us at 800-284-1114 or www.ctpub.com for more information about the C&T Teachers Program.

Library of Congress Cataloging-in-Publication Data

Rymer, Cyndy Lyle
Quilts for guys : 15 fun projects for your favorite
    fella / edited by Cyndy Lyle Rymer.
       p. cm.
Includes index.
  ISBN 1-57120-165-3
1. Patchwork—Patterns. 2. Quilting—Patterns. 3. Patchwork quilts.
I. Title.
  TT835 .R946 2001
  745.46'041—dc21
                          00-012854

Published by C&T Publishing, Inc.
P.O. Box 1456
Lafayette, California 94549

Printed in Hong Kong
10 9 8 7 6 5 4 3 2 1

Contents

**Why You Should Make a
Quilt for Your Guy**
4

The Projects

At the Races, 6

All Paws Great and Small, 10

Bowl-a-Rama Quilt, 15

Hayden Hits the Halfpipe, 19

Hoist the Jib, 26

Little Guys Are Great, 31

The Lure of an Autumn Stream, 35

Midnight Hoop Dreams, 39

Rainbow Trout, 44

Recycled Blues, 48

San Francisco Summer Quilt, 51

Swimming Upstream, 53

Tie Guy Quilt, 56

Timberline Trails, 64

What a Novel Idea, 68

A Few of His Favorite Things, 74

Sewing Basics
76

Resources
78

Index
80

Why You Should Make a Quilt for Your Guy

The projects in this book are for the wonderful man, or men, in your life who deserve a quilt. A quilt is a perfect gift because it comes from the heart, and is the most comforting present you can give him.

You don't have to wait for a special occasion such as a birthday or graduation to make a quilt for your guy. Your desire to present him with a reminder of your love and creativity is good enough reason to dedicate the time and patience it takes to create any quilt. The quilts chosen for this book were meant to be as simple as possible, and were intended to reflect as many potential interests as possible.

Hopefully there are guys out there who will pick up this book and make one of the quilts. After all, sewing machines are power tools. And so are hot irons! How about rotary cutters? They're just saws without teeth.

If your guy loves to fish, take a look at *The Lure of an Autumn Stream* on page 35, *Rainbow Trout* on page 44, or *Swimming Upstream* on page 53.

If his passion is sailing, take a look at *Hoist the Jib* on page 26. If you've never tried paper piecing, this might be a great time for your first attempt. The sailboat blocks, which float within a familiar triple Irish chain pattern, are relatively easy to paper piece.

For the guy who is into cars or motorcycles—antique, classic, funny cars, monster trucks, etc.—*At the Races* is a fun and doable project that incorporates both piecing and fusible appliqué. You can use all of the appliqués, use the ones that your guy would love, or add your own.

Many of the projects are intended to be wallhangings that will make even the most drab office space feel cozier, or they can hang in a place of honor in a hunting or fishing lodge. There are some that would be large enough to wrap up in, such as *San Francisco Summer Quilt* on page 51, *Little Guys Are Great* on page 31, *All Paws Great and Small* on page 10, *Timberline Trails* on page 64, *Recycled Blues* on page 48, and *Midnight Hoop Dreams* on page 39.

The *Bowl-a-Rama* quilt on page 15 could just as easily be made for baseball, football, soccer, golf, or windsurfing enthusiasts—you can find just about any sport represented in the novelty fabric section of your local quilt store. The possibilities for customizing your quilt with novelty fabrics are endless!

Recycled Blues is a great way to use those castoff blue jeans and flannel shirts that you have stashed away, especially if there is one pair of jeans or a shirt that

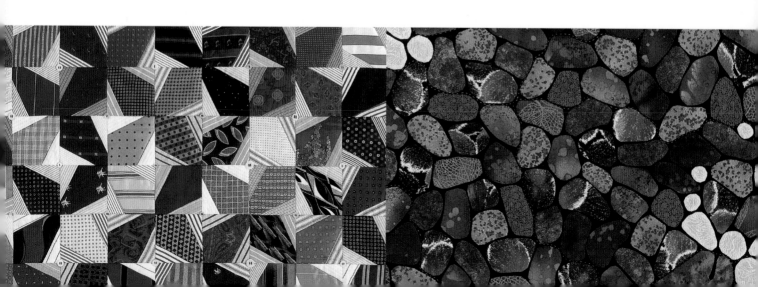

holds special memories. If the quilt ends up on the back of his favorite chair or couch, the pockets can be used to store the remote control, or you can leave him messages.

If you are looking for a great fundraiser quilt, take a look at the largest quilt in the book made by C&T author Wendy Hill and a group of volunteers: *The Tie Guy Quilt*, which is awesome in so many ways. Making this quilt was an amazing feat: first the volunteers who worked on this quilt collected over 350 ties, and then spent many, many hours taking the ties apart so they could make the blocks. Truly a labor of love, but, as you can see on page 56, well worth the effort. You or your group do not have to make such a large quilt; Wendy kindly wrote instructions for a variety of sizes from king to a small wallhanging.

Oh those wonderful novelty fabrics! We could have spent many more hours playing with all of the novelty fabrics we collected from generous fabric manufacturers and while we were on the prowl in many quilt shops. We had so much fun putting together the sample blocks in the chapter "What a Novel Idea," and in the quilt on page 74, *A Few of His Favorite Things*.

If you are making quilts for guys, let us know about them! Send photos!

guys vs. men

The following definition of guys versus men is reprinted through the courtesy of Jay Richards, one of the best guys on the C&T staff.

Don't confuse "guys" with "men" or "males." The guy is a subset of male, and may or may not be a man. Steve Young is probably the ultimate example of someone who is both a guy and a man. Anyone who is a guy but not a man isn't famous. Guys start projects. Men finish them. Guys go to the football game; men organize the tailgate party. Men can make Eggs Benedict. Guys drink beer, preferably with other guys. Men drink many things, even Cosmos, a pink drink. Guys send e-mails; men send attachments. Guys don't waste time trying to be "a better man," but a man will always try to be "just one of the guys."

I was left with just one question for Jay: So the males who go to quilt shows—are they guys or men?

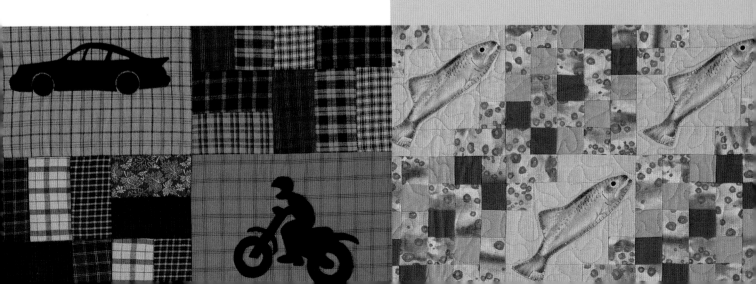

at the races

Janet Jones Worley, Huntsville, AL

Quilt Size: 52½" square

Finished Block Size: 8" x 10"

this is a fun quilt for car or racing enthusiasts. Use the cars and trucks offered, or customize it with your own. More sophisticated coloring books are a good source for a variety of car shapes.

I chose to use homespun plaids, but many different fabrics would work just as well. Remember when choosing the background fabrics for the appliqué blocks to use a fabric that will allow the black appliqué cars and trucks to pop out.

Fabric Requirements

- Plaids: 2 yards total of various light and dark colors
- Black: ⅝ yard for appliqué
- Burgundy print for border and binding: 1⅝ yards
- Backing: 3¼ yards
- Fusible adhesive web: 1½ yards
- Batting: 56" square

Cutting Instructions

Blocks

For each pieced block cut two 2½" x 4½" rectangles from each of five different plaids. You will make 10 blocks.

For each appliquéd block cut an 8½" x 10½" rectangle from each light plaid. You will make 10 blocks.

Borders

Cut two 6½" x 40½" lengthwise strips for sides, and two 6½" x 52½" lengthwise strips for top and bottom borders.

Pieced Block Assembly

Make 10 blocks total. Refer to the photo for color placement.

1. Sew three rectangles together for Unit A. Press. Make two A units for each block.

Sew two rectangles together for Unit B. Press. Make two B units for each block.

2. Sew blocks together as shown. Press.

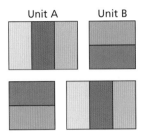

Unit A   Unit B

Preparation for Appliqué

1. Enlarge patterns on pages 8-9. Refer to the instructions on page 77 for using fusible web for appliqué. Position the various shapes on the 10½" x 8½" rectangles.

Fuse in place following the manufacturer's instructions. Appliqué the edges by hand or machine using a small zigzag, satin stitch, or buttonhole stitch.

2. Referring to the photo, sew the blocks together in rows. Press. Sew the rows together. Press.

Borders

Attach the side border strips, then the top and bottom border strips. Press seams toward border.

NOTE:
All patterns need to be
enlarged 135%.

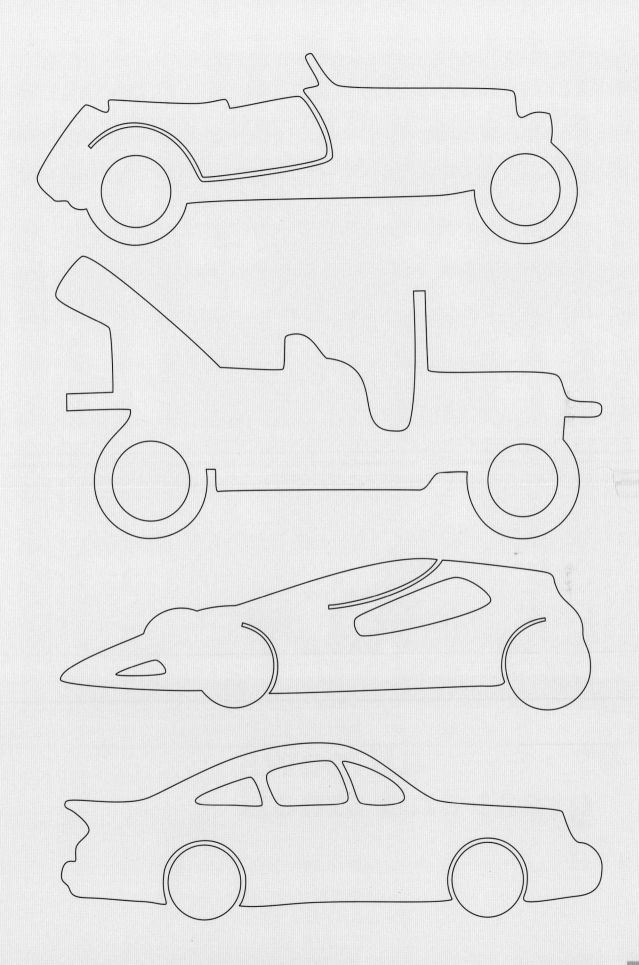

all paws
great and small

Maureen Horne, Pleasant Hill, CA

Quilt Size: 96½" square

Finished Block Size: 14"

Finished Mini Bear Paw Block Size: 4"

i wanted to make a striking two-color quilt and chose very pale blue and dark blue fabrics. This was made for my teenage nephew, so to make it more masculine I used the dark as the dominant color (background) and the light for the paws and bears.

When planning your quilt you may want to sketch different arrangements and combinations of the blocks and see what you like. Many interesting patterns are possible! Also note that you can use the Mini Bear Paws insets, but do not need to place them within every regular paw. Secondary patterns can be formed by using the mini-paws on only two of the four paws in the block.

Fabric Tips

I suggest using light and dark fabrics for strong contrast, although this quilt would also be great done in scraps.

Fabric Requirements

- Dark blue (includes binding): 9⅝ yards
- Light blue (or white): 4⅛ yards
- Backing: 8½ yards
- Batting: 100" square

Cutting Instructions

I suggest cutting the sashing, borders, and binding strips first so leftover pieces can be used to construct the blocks.

Dark Blue

Cut twelve 14½" squares for setting squares.

Cut four 6½"-wide strips for D; from two of these strips, cut twenty-six 2½" x 6½" pieces. Set aside remaining strips.

Cut four 14½"-wide strips, then cut into sixty 2½" x 14½" strips for sashing.

Cut ten 4½"-wide strips; piece end to end and cut two 88½"-long strips and two 96½"-long strips for the outside border.

Cut ten 2¼"-wide strips; piece end to end for binding.

Light Blue or White

Cut four 4½"-wide strips, then cut into thirty-two 4½" squares for C.

Cut one 2½"-wide strip for E.

Cut three 2½"-wide strips, then cut into thirty-six 2½" squares for cornerstones.

Cut nine 1½"-wide strips; piece end to end and cut into two 82½"-long strips and two 84½"-long strips for the inner border.

NOTE:
The remaining fabric will be used to make half-square triangle units and for paper piecing.

Block Assembly

Making Half-Square Triangles

Make 208 2½" half-square triangles (A) for 13 Bear Paw blocks.

Make 172 2½" half-square triangles (A) for the Sawtooth border. For ease in construction, the number of half-square triangles differs from the quilt photographed.

The half-square triangles (A) used in the regular-sized paws and Sawtooth border are easy to make using a product such as Triangles on a Roll™ or Thangles™ (2" finished square size). You can also draw your own triangle paper following the diagram provided, or you can draw the grid directly on the light fabric.

Each grid square makes two half-square triangles. To keep the size of the grid manageable, I recommend the fabric pieces be no wider than 18". Also, leave ¼" or so of fabric around the edges.

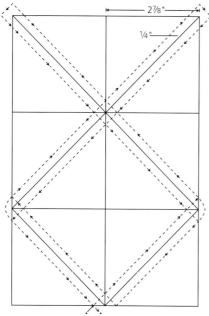

Grid for 12 half-square triangles (A) for Bear Paws and Sawtooth border

Working with Triangle Paper

1. Stack your two fabrics right sides together. Pin the triangle paper, printed side up, to the wrong side of the top fabric.

2. Using a small stitch length, stitch on the dotted lines only. A smaller stitch will perforate the paper and make it easier to remove later. Begin at an exterior point and stitch continuously along the dotted line, pivoting the fabric at the corners. The fabric outside of the grid will be cut off, so it's fine to sew there to bridge between dotted lines.

3. Cut on the solid lines to form the triangle-squares.

4. Tear off paper and discard.

5. Press blocks open, with seams toward dark fabric. Trim.

Regular Paws Block

The regular paws block and block with mini-paws are identical except the colors are reversed, and the Mini Bear Paws blocks are paper pieced. Instructions for making them are on page 13.

For each block:

1. Sew two As together as shown to form Unit A. Press seam toward the darker fabric. Make 4.

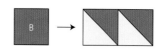

Unit A

2. Add corner square B to Unit A. Press seam toward B.

3. Sew two half-square triangle units together in the opposite direction, as shown, to form Unit B, which is a mirror image of Unit A. Press seam toward darker fabric. Make 4.

Unit B

4. Attach a large light square (C) to each Unit B. Press the seam toward the large square.

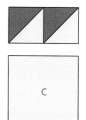

NOTE: You can substitute the mini-paw unit in place of square C.

5. Following the diagram, sew the two units together. Press toward the large square. Make 4.

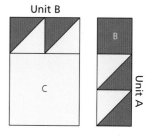

6. Make two stacks of paws as shown. Take one paw from the left-hand stack and sew on strip D following the diagram. Press the seam toward D. Add a paw from the other stack, again pressing seam toward D. Make two sets for each block.

7. To strip piece Unit D/E sew a 2½" strip of light between two 6½" strips of dark. Press the seams toward the dark strips, then cut 2½"-wide pieces as shown.

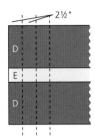

8. Arrange the paw sets as shown. Sew the paws to the center strip. Press the seams toward the center strip. Make eight blocks. The block should measure 14½" including seam allowance.

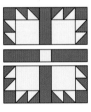

Mini Bear Paw Insets

Please note that the colors are reversed in the Mini Bear Paw block, and that you must make sixteen units for each block.

The pieces forming the Mini Paws are unusual sizes and very small. Paper piecing these blocks will avoid cutting and trying to sew the tiny pieces and form accurate points. Copy the paper-piecing patterns found on page 14. Refer to the paper-piecing instructions on page 77.

Follow Steps 1-4 above to make the large paw. Substitute a Mini Paw block for square C in Step 5. Follow Steps 6-9. Make five large paw blocks with the Mini Paw insets.

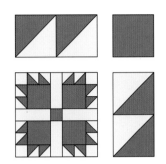

Sashing/Cornerstones

I used dark sashing (cut 2½" wide) between the blocks to blend with the background. The cornerstones (cut 2½" square) are light fabric and stand out like the paws.

1. Stitch Bear Paws blocks together, setting squares and sashing in rows, referring to the photo for placement. Press.

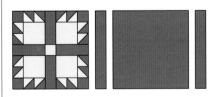

NOTE: When sewing the sashing to the block, you may want to place the pieced block on top so you can see the seam cross-points and avoid cutting off the tips of the paws.

2. Stitch the sashing and corner-stones together in rows as shown. Press. Make six rows.

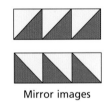

3. Stitch block rows and sashing rows together, referring to the photo for placement. Press.

Borders

Inner Border

Sew the inner border strips to sides of quilt. Press. Repeat for the top and bottom border. Press.

Sawtooth Border

Sew 42 half-square triangles (A) together into strips, dividing the strip in half so the right half is a mirror image of the left half. Add to sides of quilt. Press.

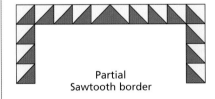

Mirror images

Partial
Sawtooth border

Sew 44 half-square triangles (A) together as above and add to top and bottom of quilt. Press.

Outer Border

Sew outer border strips to sides of quilt. Press. Repeat for the top and bottom borders. Press.

Quilting

Following is a description of my quilting plan.

Solid block: a circular design centered in the block.

Regular Paws block: straight diagonal lines parallel to the lines in the triangle-squares; also outlined the center strips and square ¼" in from the seams.

Bear Paws block with Mini Bear Paws inset: stitch in-the-ditch to outline the large paws and the tiny center square in each quadrant; outline the center strips and square ¼" in from the seams.

Sashing and cornerstones: stitch in-the-ditch along all seams of the sashing and cornerstones between the blocks. Straight lines are quilted, forming X's in each post and two stretched X's in each sash.

Border: stitch in-the-ditch along the outer edge only of the Sawtooth border. An interlocking design adapted from a stencil was used in the outer border.

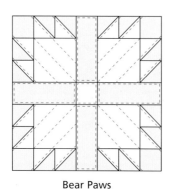

Bear Paws

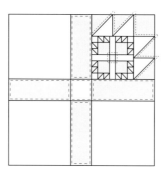

Bear Paws with Mini Bear Paw

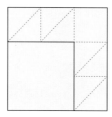

Paw Outline

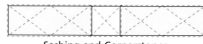

Sashing and Cornerstones

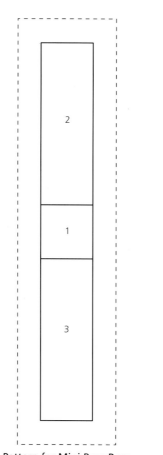

Pattern for Mini Bear Paw
Make 20 copies.

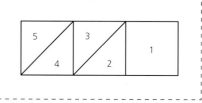

Pattern for Mini Bear Paw
Make 40 copies.

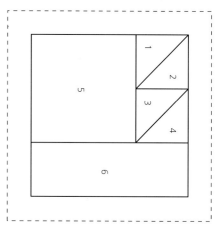

Pattern for Mini Bear Paw
Make 40 copies.

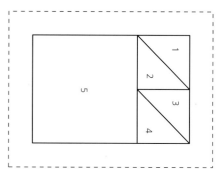

Pattern for Mini Bear Paw
Make 40 copies.

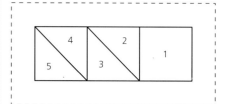

Pattern for Mini Bear Paw
Make 40 copies.

bowl-a-rama quilt

Michele Crawford, Spokane, WA

Quilt Size: 46½" square

made as a market sample for Classsic Cottons, this quilt is a perfect strike! While the bowler you live with would appreciate this quilt, the pattern could be adapted to be used with any of the coordinated novelty prints currently available. If preprinted panels aren't available in the fabrics of your choice, make more pinwheel blocks for the center, or add a photo transfer block of your guy in action, or...

Fabric Requirements

All fabrics are from Classic Cotton's "Bowl-A-Rama" collection.

- Preprinted Bowler Panel
- Bowlers print: ¼ yard
- Bowling shoes print: ⅝ yard
- Bowling balls print (includes binding): ⅔ yard
- Red marble swirl: ⅝ yard
- Blue marble swirl: ⅛ yard
- White: ½ yard
- Black: ¼ yard
- Gold print: ¼ yard
- Backing: 3 yards
- Batting: 51" square
- Fusible adhesive web: ⅝ yard
- Embroidery floss: 1 skein red
- 4 buttons (JHB Buttons: 2 white bowling pins, 2 black bowling balls)

Cutting Instructions

Red marble swirl:
Sashing strips: Cut eight 1½"-wide strips, then cut into four 1½" x 34½" strips, four 1½" x 16½" strips, and eight 1½" x 8½" strips.

Cut two 6¼" squares, then cut in half diagonally twice to make eight quarter-square triangles.

Blue marble swirl for corner squares:
Cut eight 1½" squares.

Bowlers print:
Cut four 8½" squares.

Bowling balls print:
Cut eight 4½" squares and sixteen 2⅞" squares. Cut smaller squares in half diagonally to make 32 half-square triangles.

Gold print:
Cut sixteen 2⅞" squares, then cut squares in half diagonally to make 32 half-square triangles.

Black:
Cut four 8½" squares.

White:
Cut two 6¼" squares, then cut in half diagonally twice to make eight quarter-square triangles.

Preprinted bowler panel:
Cut one 16½" square for quilt center.

Bowling shoes print for borders:
Cut four 5½" x 36½" strips.

Quilt Assembly

Pinwheel Blocks

1. Make 32 half-square triangles by sewing a bowling ball triangle to a gold print triangle. Press.

Make 32.

2. Sew four half-square triangle units together to make a 4½" pinwheel block. Press. Make 8 pinwheel blocks.

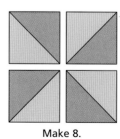

Make 8.

3. Sew a 4½" bowling ball print square to each pinwheel square. Press.

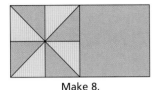
Make 8.

4. Noting the direction of bowlers print, sew a bowling balls/pinwheel unit to the top and bottom of two bowlers print squares, and to the sides of the two other bowlers print squares. Press.

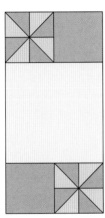
Make 2.

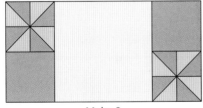
Make 2.

Bowling Pin Blocks

Refer to the instructions on page 77 for using fusible web for appliqué.

1. Cut four 8" x 14" white rectangles and fuse two layers together. (Note: Two layers of white fabric are used for the bowling pins to avoid show-through of the black background square.) For the bowling balls, cut a 3½" x 14" rectangle of blue marble swirl.

2. Trace the bowling pins pattern twice on fusible web. Then reverse the pattern and trace two more pins. Place on double layer of the fused white fabric and cut out pieces.

3. Trace four bowling balls on fusible web, place on the blue marble swirl fabric, and cut out all the pieces.

4. Center bowling pins and a ball in each black square. Fuse the pieces to the black square following the manufacturer's instructions.

5. With white thread, machine appliqué the bowling pins using a satin stitch. Use a medium blue thread to machine appliqué the balls.

6. Use six strands of red floss to sew three straight stitches across the neck of each bowling pin (as shown on the pattern).

7. Sew the blocks, sashing strips, and corner squares together as shown. Press. The quilt top should now measure 36½" square including seam allowance.

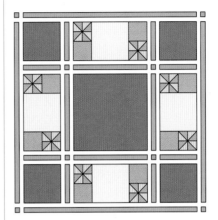

Borders

1. Sew the red marble swirl triangles together with the white triangles as shown to make the outside border corner squares. Press.

Make 4.

2. Sew the bowling shoes border strips to the sides of the quilt. Sew a red and white quarter-square triangle square to each end of the remaining border strips and sew to the top and bottom of the quilt.

Quilting

Stitch in-the-ditch in all of the seams of the quilt.

Embellishing

Sew a bowling pin button in the center of the top right and lower left pieced outside border square. Sew a bowling ball button in the center of the top left and lower right pieced outside border square.

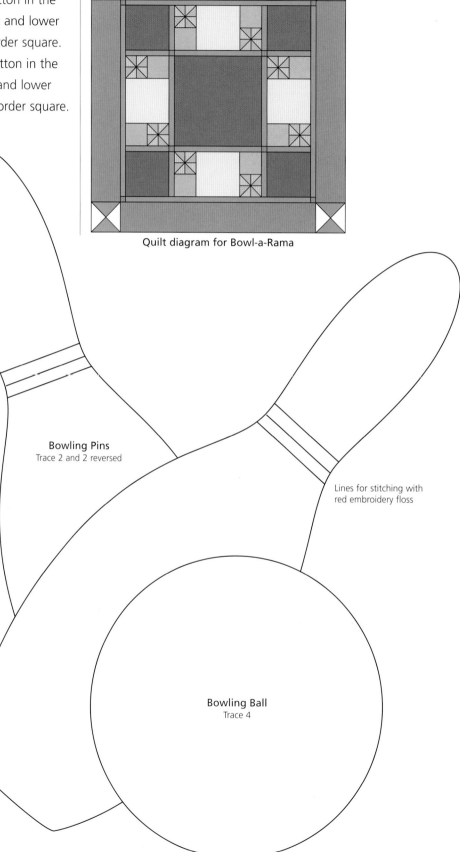

Quilt diagram for Bowl-a-Rama

Bowling Pins
Trace 2 and 2 reversed

Lines for stitching with red embroidery floss

Bowling Ball
Trace 4

hayden hits
the halfpipe

Judith Hughes Marte, Nine Mile Falls, WA

Size of Quilt: 64" x 82"

i made this quilt for my ten-year old son, Hayden, who loves to snowboard. The "halfpipe" is an area at the ski resort where boarders can do tricks. My goal was to capture Hayden "catching some air" as he enjoys a day on the slopes of eastern Washington near our home.

Fabric Tips

Rather than choosing just one light fabric for the sky and one or two dark fabrics for the mountainsides, I chose a variety of fabrics to add more interest and movement to the quilt. I used a number of light blue fabrics for the sky with subtle clouds, swirls, and snowflakes. A variety of greens and blues with stripes, swirls, and streaks were used for the mountainsides. I wanted the quilt to have the feeling of a snowy day without having it be predominantly white (remember, this quilt is for a ten-year-old boy!). I repeated the red and yellow in the snowboarder appliqué in the border and sun to give the quilt some spark.

I used fusible web for the snowboarder and other appliqués and embellished with machine satin stitching and top-stitching.

Fabric Requirements

- Blue with clouds: ¾ yard for center rectangle
- Five light blue sky prints for sky and second border: ¼ yard of each
- One additional light blue sky print for sky and second border: ⅓ yard
- Green print for one mountain: ⅓ yard
- Three additional green prints for mountainsides and second border: ¼ yard of each
- Five blue prints for mountainsides and second border: ¼ yard of each

- Blue print for third border and mountainsides: 1¾ yards
- Red for first border: ¼ yard
- Scraps of your choice for snowboarder, sun, mountaintop, and snowflake appliqué
- Fusible adhesive web: 2 yards
- Backing: 5 yards
- Binding: ⅝ yard black print
- Batting: 86" x 68"
- Black, golden-orange, and white threads for satin stitching

Cutting and Assembly Instructions

Section 1: Center Rectangle for Snowboarder Appliqué

Cut one 30½" x 23½" rectangle from blue fabric with clouds.

Snowboarder Appliqué

NOTE:
Before fusing, layer shapes as shown in the diagram on page 22. For example, the right sleeve of the jacket is placed under the right pants leg, and part of the lower glove is placed under the snowboard.

Enlarge the snowboarder appliqué shapes 200%. Follow the instructions on page 77 for fusible appliqué and fuse the shapes onto the center rectangle.

Outline all pieces of the appliqué design with a machine satin stitch using black thread. Also use a satin stitch to make additional detail lines on the ski jacket and pants as indicated on the pattern pieces.

Sections 2, 3, 4, and 5

Refer to the cutting diagrams given. All measurements shown are the cut sizes. The measurements given for all triangles are the size to cut a square; when the square is cut in half diagonally it will yield the triangle needed. The diagrams indicate the colors for each piece.

Sew these sections following the construction diagrams. Always join half-square triangles into squares before sewing these to other pieces.

Section 2: Cut and assemble as shown. Press. Completed section will measure 12½" x 30½" including seam allowance.

Section 3: Cut and assemble as shown. Press. Completed section will measure 12½" x 30½" including seam allowance.

Section 4: Cut and assemble as shown. Press. Completed section will measure 47½" x 14½" including seam allowance.

Section 5: Cut and assemble as shown. Press. Completed section will measure 47½" x 21½" including seam allowance.

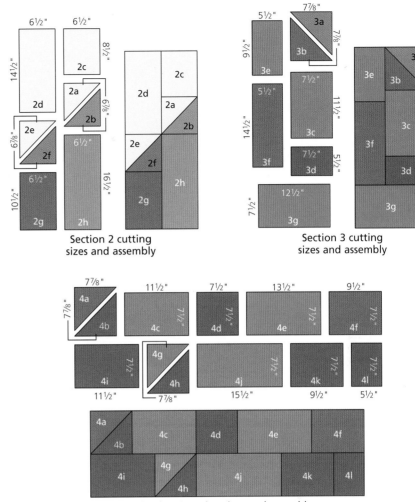

Section 2 cutting sizes and assembly

Section 3 cutting sizes and assembly

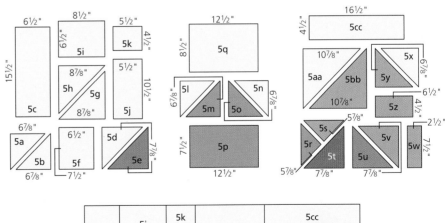

Section 4 cutting sizes and assembly

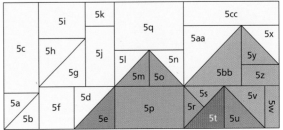

Section 5 cutting sizes and assembly

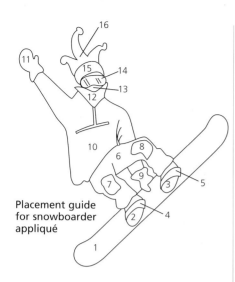

Placement guide
for snowboarder
appliqué

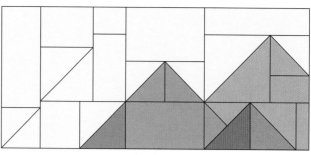

Section 5

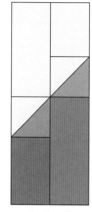

Section 2   Section 1   Section 3

Section 4

Quilt Top Assembly

Sew Section 2 to the left side of
Section 1. Press.

Sew Section 3 to the right side
of Section 1. Press.

Sew Section 4 to the bottom
of Sections 1, 2, and 3. Press.

Sew Section 5 to the top of sections 1, 2 & 3. Press. The quilt top
should now measure 47½" x 65½"
including seam allowances.

Borders

First Border

Cut six 1¼"-wide strips of red
fabric and piece end to end.

From this strip cut two 65½" strips
for side borders and two 49" strips
for the top and bottom borders.
Sew borders to sides and then to
the top and bottom of quilt. Press.

Second Border

Cut one 3⅜" square of sky fabric,
then cut in half diagonally.

Cut one 3⅜" square of green fabric, then cut in half diagonally.

Cut 3"-wide strips of assorted 5"
to 15" lengths from the sky, green,
and blue fabrics. These will be
joined into the necessary lengths
for each border.

Left Side Second Border

1. Join one sky triangle and one
green triangle to form a
3" square (including
seam allowances). Press.

2. Join assorted 3"-wide sky fabric
strips to a 45" length and sew this
to the top of the 3" half-square
triangle unit. Press.

3. Join assorted 3"-wide green and blue fabrics to a 27" length and sew this to the bottom of the square. Press.

4. Sew this border piece to the left side of the quilt top. Press. This border strip should line up so the green half-square triangle extends the line of the mountainside created by piece 2f in Section 2. Trim each end to fit.

Right Side Second Border

1. Join one sky triangle and one green triangle to form a 3" square (including seam allowances). Press.

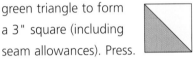

2. Join assorted 3"-wide sky fabric strips for a total length of 14" and sew this to the top of the 3" half-square triangle unit—the sky triangle—refer to quilt photograph). Press.

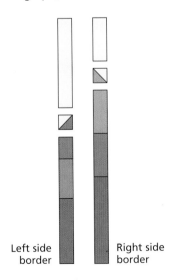

Left side border   Right side border

3. Join assorted green and blue 3"-wide strips to a total length of

55" and sew this to the bottom of the 3" square (the green triangle). Sew this border piece to the right side of the quilt top. Press. Again, the green triangle should line up so it extends the line of triangle piece 5y in Section 5. Trim each end to fit.

Top and Bottom Second Border

1. For the top piece, join assorted 3"-wide sky fabrics to a total length of 54" and sew this to the top of the quilt. Press.

2. For the bottom piece, join assorted 3"-wide green and blue fabrics to total 54" and sew this to the bottom of the quilt. Press.

Third Border

Cut eight 5½"-wide strips of blue border fabric and piece end to end. From this length cut two 72" side border strips and two 64" top and bottom strips.

Sew borders to the sides and then to the top and bottom of the quilt.

Sun, Mountaintop, and Snowflake Appliqués

Make enlargements of the pattern pieces on pages 24-25. Make three mountaintops with white fabrics. Make the sun using the five pattern pieces and assorted yellow fabrics. Make the following snowflakes from assorted white fabrics: 1 small, 2 medium, and 2 large of Pattern A, and 2 small, 3 medium, and 1 large of Pattern B.

Fuse mountaintops, sun, and snowflakes to the quilt top, referring to the photograph for placement. Use a satin stitch to outline the sun with golden-orange thread and the mountain tops with black thread. On the snowflakes, use white thread and a straight stitch to topstitch just inside all edges.

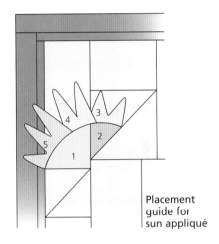

Placement guide for sun appliqué

Binding

Cut eight 2½"-wide strips of black print and piece end to end.

Quilting

I stitched in-the-ditch around the center rectangle and along the first and second borders. Curved lines were used to accentuate the path of the snowflake appliqués. I free-motion quilted cloud-like and swirl shapes in the sky area. In the mountainside areas I added some parallel straight lines (using masking tape as a sewing guide) and some free-motion quilting following the curved lines in the fabric designs.

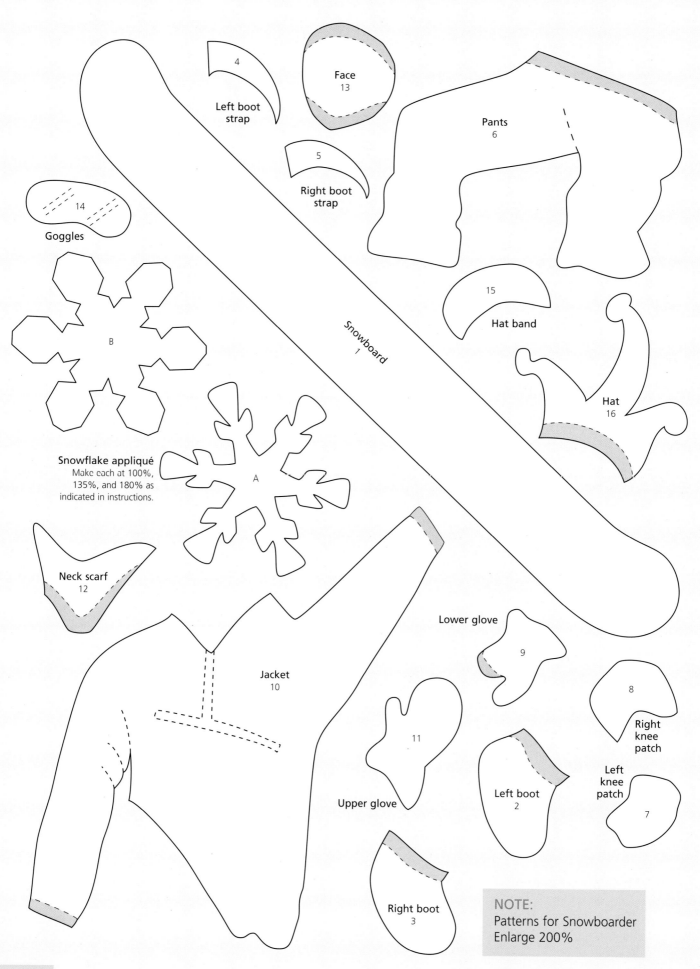

4

Left boot
strap

Face
13

Pants
6

5

Right boot
strap

14

Goggles

15

Hat band

Snowboard
1

Hat
16

B

Snowflake appliqué
Make each at 100%,
135%, and 180% as
indicated in instructions.

A

Neck scarf
12

Lower glove

9

8

Jacket
10

Right
knee
patch

11

Left
knee
patch

7

Upper glove

Left boot
2

Right boot
3

NOTE:
Patterns for Snowboarder
Enlarge 200%

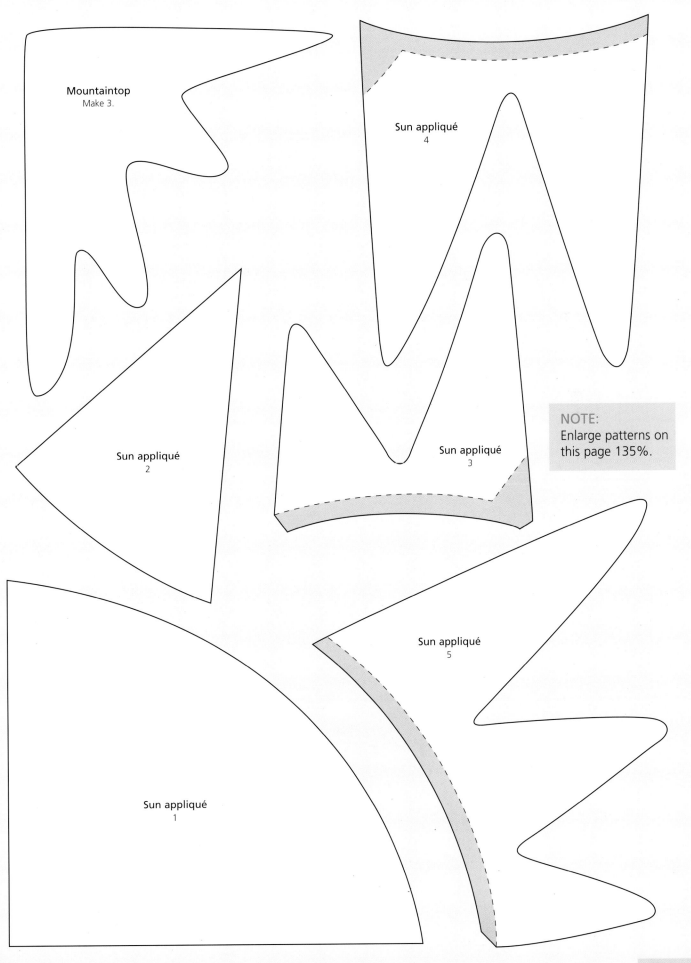

Mountaintop
Make 3.

Sun appliqué
4

Sun appliqué
2

Sun appliqué
3

NOTE:
Enlarge patterns on
this page 135%.

Sun appliqué
5

Sun appliqué
1

hoist the jib

Pat Rose, Orinda, CA

Quilt Size: 79" X 107"

Finished Block Size: 14"

this quilt captures the feeling of peace and tranquility felt while skipping across the water on one of those million-dollar days when the sky is a perfect azure blue and the sun's rays warm you to the core. The bright nautical colors used in the Flying Geese border and the paper-pieced sailboats combined with the soothing sea and cloud blues create a quilt that will never grow dull or out-of-date, and is bound to please the sailor in your life.

Fabric Tips

Check your stash for cloud-like and watery blues that trigger those wonderful memories of blissful days spent at the beach.

Fabric Requirements

- Assorted medium blues for blocks: 1 yard total
- Light medium blue cloud-print I for blocks: 2½ yards
- Light medium blue cloud-print II for blocks: 1¼ yards
- Solid light blue for blocks, boats, and Flying Geese backgrounds: 4½ yards
- White for ship and flying geese: 1 yard
- Seven to eight different solid brights for geese and ships: ¼ yard of each
- Cloud-print in light or medium blue for outer border: 1 yard
- Medium blue for binding: ⅔ yard
- Backing: 7 yards
- Batting: 83" x 111"

Cutting

Blocks

All strips are cut 42" long (or by the width of the fabric).

Medium blue:
Cut twenty-two 2½"-wide strips.

Light medium blue I:
Cut thirty-one 2½"-wide strips.

Light medium blue II:
Cut sixteen 2½"-wide strips.

Light blue:
Cut six 2½"-wide strips and three 10½"-wide strips. Cut eight 6½"-wide strips. From five of the 6½"-wide strips cut thirty-four 4½" x 6½" rectangles.

Outer Border

Cloud fabric:
Cut ten 2¾"-wide strips. Piece together end to end and cut two 102½" strips for side outer borders and two 79" strips for top and bottom borders.

Binding

Medium blue:
Cut ten 2¼"-wide strips.

Block Assembly

Block A

Block A
Make 18.

NOTE:
To make the strip sets: cut one to three 2½"-wide strips from each color to make the number of 42"-long and 21"-long strip sets needed.

1. For strip set A1 (Row 1) sew two medium blue, two light medium blue I, two light medium blue II, and one light blue 2½"-wide strips in the order shown to make two 42"-long strip sets and one 21"-long strip set. Press and cut into thirty-six 2½"-wide segments.

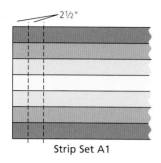

Strip Set A1

2. For strip set A2 (Row 2) sew two medium blue, four light medium blue I, and one light medium blue II 2½"-wide strips in the order shown to make two 42"-long strip sets and one 21"-long strip set. Press and cut into thirty-six 2½"-wide segments.

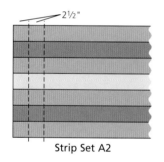

Strip Set A2

3. For strip set A3 (Row 3) sew two medium blue, three light medium blue I, and two light medium blue II strips in the order shown to make two 42"-long strip sets and one 21"-long strip set. Press and cut into thirty-six 2½"-wide segments.

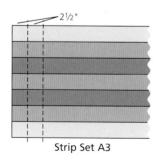

Strip Set A3

4. For strip set A4 (Row 4) sew one medium blue, two light medium blue I, two light medium blue II, and two light blue 2½"-wide strips in the order shown to make one 42"-long strip set and one 21"-long strip set. Press and cut into eighteen 2½"-wide segments.

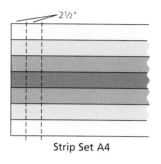

Strip Set A4

5. Stitch strip set segments together in order shown—Row 1, Row 2, Row 3, Row 4, Row 3, Row 2, Row 1. Press. Make 18 Block A's.

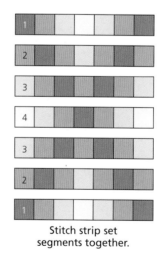

Stitch strip set segments together.

Block B: Paper-Pieced Ships

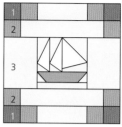

Block B Make 17.

To make the ships, make seventeen copies of the paper-piecing pattern on page 30 and follow the directions for paper piecing on page 77. Use assorted brights for the ship, white for the sails, and light blue for the background. Make 17 ships.

You will need to cut one set of fabric strips in half for one short strip set each.

1. To make strip set B1 (Row 1) sew two medium blue 2½"-wide strips, two light medium blue I 2½"-wide strips, and one light blue 6½" wide strip in the order shown to make to make two 42"-long strip sets and one 21"-long strip set. Press and cut into thirty-four 2½"-wide segments for Row 1.

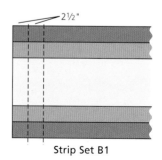

Strip Set B1

2. To make strip set B2 (Row 2) sew two light medium blue I 2½"-wide strips to each side of a light blue 10½"-wide strip as shown to make two 42"-long strip sets and one 21"-long strip set. Press and cut into thirty-four 2½" segments for Row 2.

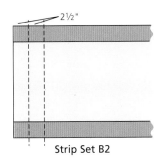

Strip Set B2

3. Sew a 4½" x 6½" light blue rectangle to each side of the ship block for Row 3 as shown. Press.

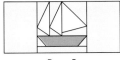

Row 3

4. Sew strip set segments together with Row 3 as shown. Press. Make 17 blocks.

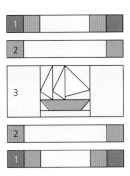

Quilt Assembly

Stitch blocks A and B together in rows as shown. Press. Stitch rows together as shown. Press.

Flying Geese Border

Make 58 copies for the Flying Geese paper-piecing pattern on page 30. (You may wish to piece together more than one segment of six geese to make longer rows of geese.) Follow the paper-piecing directions on page 77. Use assorted bright colors for geese and light blue for background. Stitch geese end to end to make two rows of 98 each for side borders and two rows of 74 each for top and bottom borders. Press.

Outer Border

Sew 102½"-long strips to the sides of the quilt, and 79"-long strips to the top and bottom. Press.

Quilting

I used an overall meandering quilting pattern.

Note: All solid blocks are Block A. Actual number of Flying Geese differs from diagram.

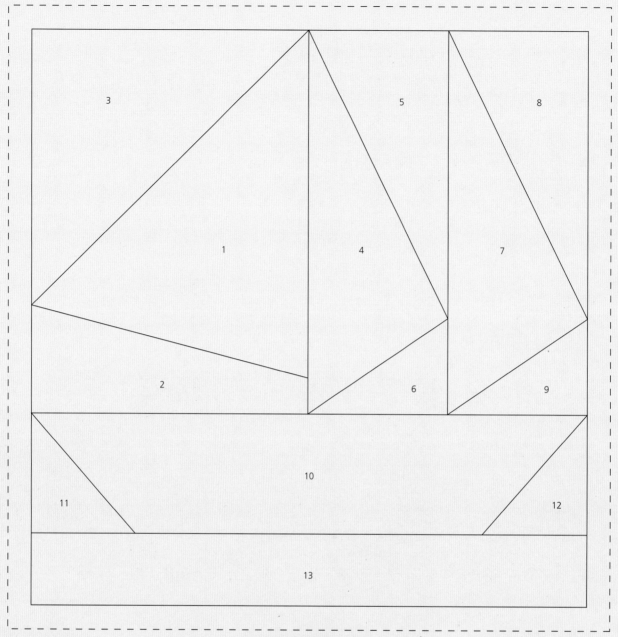

Hoist the Jib Ship Pattern
Make 17 copies.

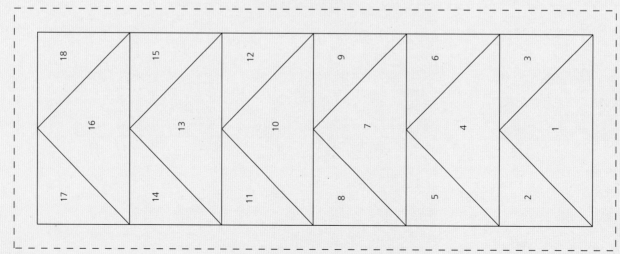

Hoist the Jib Flying Geese Border Unit Pattern
Make 58 copies.

little guys are great

Designed and pieced by Sandy Bonsib, Issaquah, WA, 1999;
machine quilted by Becky Kraus

Quilt Size: 68½" x 77½"
Finished Block Size: 9"

flannel has to be the fabric of choice when you want to make a warm and cozy quilt. This quilt is large enough that your guy can wrap himself up in it while watching the game.

Some of my students choose not to include the Little Guy blocks, so feel free to do the same, replacing them with more Square Within a Square blocks.

Fabric Tips

For the Square Within a Square blocks, choose nine of your favorite flannels, but don't feel like you have to match them perfectly. Using mismatched colors makes your quilt more interesting and vibrant. Be sure to include different values of each color.

I usually wait until my top is made to choose the border fabric, but if you have found the "perfect" border or are working with a focus fabric buy two yards.

Prewash your flannels twice before cutting them because flannel can be somewhat stretchy. Some of these squares may not look perfectly square even though you cut them exactly. Don't worry about this. You will be able to ease your squares to fit as you sew.

Fabric Requirements

All fabrics are flannels unless otherwise indicated.

- Assorted flannels for the Square Within a Square blocks and the corner blocks: 5 yards total (I bought ½ yard pieces of each flannel)
- For the Little Guy Blocks: ¼ yard for background, ⅛ yard for skin, scraps for overalls and hats
- Inner border: 1 yard
- Outer border: 1¾ yards
- Backing: 4 yards
- Binding: ⅝ yard (cotton, not flannel, for less bulk)
- Batting: 72" x 81"

Cutting Instructions

Square Within a Square Blocks

Cut eight or nine 6" squares from each ½ yard piece to create the Square Within A Square blocks. You will cut 81 squares total. Choose 27 of these for the centers of the blocks. Cut the remaining squares in half diagonally.

Little Guy Blocks
Cut for each block

Background:
Two 3½" x 4¾" (A3 and C5)
Two 3½" x 4½" (A1 and C1)
One 3½" square (C4)
One 1½" x 2½" (B10)
Two 1¼" x 2½" (B4)
Two 1¼" x 2" (B8)
Two 1" squares (B1)

Skin:
One 3½" x 1¼" (A2)
One 1¼" x 5½" (C3)
One 2" square (B3)
One 1¼" square (C2)
Four 1" squares (B2)

Hat:
One 2" square (B7) and one 1" x 3½" (B6)

Overalls:
One 3" x 3½" (B9)
Two 1½" x 2½" (B11)
Two 1" x 1¼" (B5)

Inner Border

Cut six 4"-wide strips and piece end to end.

Outer Border

Cut four 8½"-wide strips lengthwise.

Outer border corners:
Cut four 6" squares. Cut eight more 6" squares in half diagonally.

Assembly Instructions

Square Within a Square Blocks

For each block you need one center square and four triangles cut from two different flannels.

1. Sew a triangle to each side of a square.

> **TIP:**
> To find the centers for the squares and triangles, fold each square and triangle in half and finger press to form a crease. Match the creases, pin, and stitch. Press seam allowances toward the triangles; trim.

2. Add two more triangles to the remaining sides. Press the seam allowances toward the triangles.

3. Make 27 blocks. Trim all blocks to measure 9½" square.

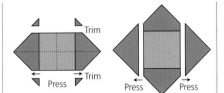

Little Guy Blocks

See diagrams below for placement of all pieces. Make three blocks.

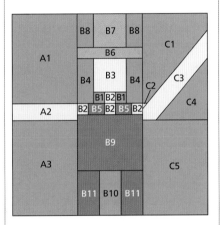

Section A: Left Arm Unit

Sew pieces A1, A2, and A3 together. Press.

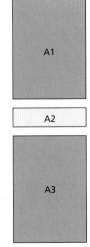

Section B: Head, Neck, and Shoulders Unit

1. Sew a piece B1 to each side of piece B2 and sew this unit to the bottom of B3. Sew a B4 piece to each side of the unit. Press.

2. Sew pieces B2, B5, B2, B5, B2 in a row. Sew this strip to the bottom of the B1-B4 unit. Press.

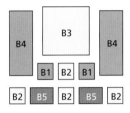

Hat Unit

Sew a piece B8 to each side of B7 and sew the row to the top of B6. Sew the unit to the top of the head and shoulders B1-B5 unit.

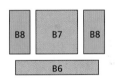

Overalls Unit

Sew a piece B11 to each side of B10 and sew the row to the bottom of B9. Sew the unit to the bottom of the head and shoulders unit.

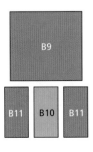

Section C: Right Arm Unit

1. Sew the 1¼" skin square (C2) to the bottom-left corner of the background rectangle (C1). Press the square away from the rectangle.

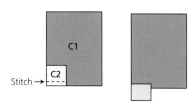

2. Mark a stitching line at a 45° angle from the lower bottom-left corner of the rectangle (C1) to the upper right side of (C1). Trim ¼" below the line.

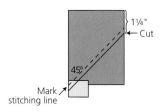

3. Sew the arm piece (C3) along this diagonal line. Press seam toward arm piece.

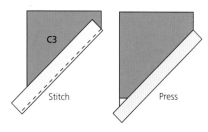

4. Place a background square (C4) on top of C1-C3 unit, matching the sides and extending to the bottom-left corner of the arm piece. Turn over and sew along the edge of the arm piece (C3) using a ¼" seam. Trim (C4) excess along the edge of the arm piece. Press the untrimmed part of C4 away from the arm. Press seam toward arm.

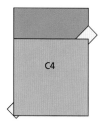

Place C4 on C1-C3 unit right sides together.

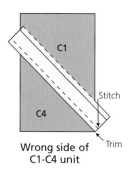

Wrong side of C1-C4 unit

5. Trim bottom and sides of unit to measure 3½" x 5¼".

Unit Assembly

Sew Units A, B, and C together and press. Trim block to measure 9½" square.

Quilt Assembly

1. Arrange all your blocks on a design wall, five across and six down.

2. Sew the blocks together in rows, alternating the direction you press the seams from row to row. Sew the rows together.

Borders

Inner Borders

1. Cut two 4"-wide strips 54½" long (or the vertical measurement for your quilt top) for the inner borders. Sew to the sides of the quilt. Press seams toward borders.

2. Cut two 4"-wide strips for the inner top and bottom borders 52½" long (or the horizontal measurement of your quilt top). Add to the top and bottom of your quilt. Press seams toward borders.

Outer Borders

1. Follow directions on page 33 to make four Square Within a Square blocks for the border corners. Trim to measure 8½" square.

2. Cut two 8½"-wide strips 61½" long (or the vertical measurement of your quilt top) for the side borders. Press seams toward borders.

Cut two 8½"-wide strips 52½" long and sew the corner blocks on each end for the top and bottom borders. Sew to the top and bottom. Press seams toward borders.

Binding

I do not use flannel on the binding because it is bulky; however, if you want to do a flannel binding, cut the strips 2¼" or 2½" rather than 2" and make the binding wider.

" crystal waters flowing by within them lie sparkling pebbles and reflections of sky "

the lure of an autumn stream

Carol Armstrong, Singleton, MI

Quilt Size: 20" x 31"

the senses are awakened by the vibrant colors full of sun, and the muted hues that rest quietly in the shadows. Moment passes moment; image passes image, each separate and brief. Life's current carries them past.

My quilts are my poems, as Haiku that speaks of one time, of one moment. A field of yellow and orange hawkweed catches the light just so, and takes your breath away. I hold in my hand sapphire blueberries and savor their warm sweetness on my tongue. The autumn-colored trees are reflected in a drop of rain at the tip of a branch but with the sky below. I want to save such things. All else retreats and I am part of the earth completely and I understand.

Fabric Tips

Subtle or very large prints, as well as hand-dyed fabrics with a lot of texture, work well for the pebbles. A large print is transformed when it is cut into a small shape.

Experiment with the painting techniques; mix colors and use silk salt on a test piece of fabric. Refer to Mickey Lawler's book *Skydyes* for more information.

"Test" your fabrics by cutting out a few pebbles of each and laying them out on the background fabric. Play until you find the combination you like.

A solid tan fabric was used as the base for the painted fish.

Fabric Requirements

- Background and backing: 1¼ yards total
- Fish: ¼ yard of a print fabric, or tan if you are going to paint with dye
- Pebbles: scraps or ⅛ yard each of four or five greens, one brown, two rusts, two reds, and one white print
- Batting: 22" x 33" thin cotton batting
- Threads: matching for appliqué, white quilting thread, white basting thread, and black thread for assembly
- Optional painting for fish: Deka® Silk flowable paints in green, brown, and red; I mixed several other colors so they blended well with my pebble fabrics.
- Deka Silk Salt or coarse salt (⅛" to ¼" diameter)
- Acrylic craft paints: white, black, and metallic gold
- Stiff paint brushes meant for acrylic paints
- Freezer paper or other waterproof material to paint on

Cutting Instructions

Background and backing: cut each 22" x 33".

Enlarge the fish patterns on page 38 and cut, adding ¼" seam allowance.

Cut pebbles in a variety of similar sizes; add ¼" seam allowance to each pebble. See sample pebbles on the next page.

Assembly Instructions

1. Using a white marker, mark an 18½" x 29½" rectangle centered on the back of the background fabric. Baste with white thread on the marked line. The basting provides guidelines for placement of the appliqué shapes.

2. Appliqué the fish first. Clip the inside curves to ease turning under and needle-turn as you sew. Use a few pins or baste to hold the fish in place as you appliqué. Refer to the photo for placement.

3. Now fill in the rest of the area with pebbles. The basic pattern is random with these exceptions: a cluster of white medium size "bubbles" is sewn at each fish's mouth; some smaller white "bubbles" rise from these and at the tails. This is the only place white is used. I confined the use of the deepest red to the underside of each fish along the belly to reflect the color in the fish. The greens, rusts, and other red are used randomly.

Use your needle to turn under the seam allowance as you sew. There is no need to mark the exact size of each pebble unless you find it helpful. Leave a small space between all the pebbles like "grouting." You will find a rhythm after a while. Appliqué all the areas with the pebbles but stay within the basted line.

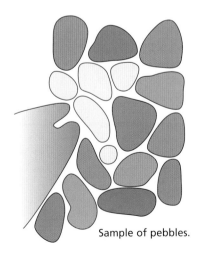
Sample of pebbles.

4. Press the appliquéd piece from the back on a soft surface, such as a towel, to prevent flattening it. Trim the piece 1¼" outside of the basting line, creating a 21" x 32" rectangle. Lay the batting down and place the backing on top with the right side up. Lay the top with the right side facing the backing and pin along the edge.

Using a ½" seam, sew the layers together, leaving an opening in the center of the bottom. Trim the seam allowance and batting to ¼" and trim the corners. Remove the basting.

Turn right-side out and press. Hand-stitch the opening closed. Baste for quilting. Quilt using white thread around each trout, and quilt in a wandering random pattern around the pebbles to hold the layers together. Add as much quilting as you like.

Optional Fabric Painting for the Fish

Using the patterns on page 38, cut out an overly large fish from a prewashed 100% cotton fabric. Wet the fabric and lay out on some freezer paper or another type of non-absorbent, disposable surface. I painted both fish at the same time to keep my mixed colors the same.

Keep the work wet, and do a test on a scrap first if you are new to fabric painting. I mixed the colors to blend with the fabrics for the pebbles. Deka silk paints are a thin dye and will flow in the wet cotton. When you find the color you like, sprinkle lightly with Deka silk salt and leave it on until the salt dries. Brush the salt off. Allow the fabric to dry completely.

Heat set the paint according to the instructions on the package. Using a stiff brush, flick dots and spots of black, white, and metallic gold acrylic craft paint onto the surface—practice this technique on a scrap first. Flick lightly for a subtle effect. Allow the paint to dry and heat set from the back of the fabric. Note that the thickness of the acrylic paint will affect the size and spread of the dots.

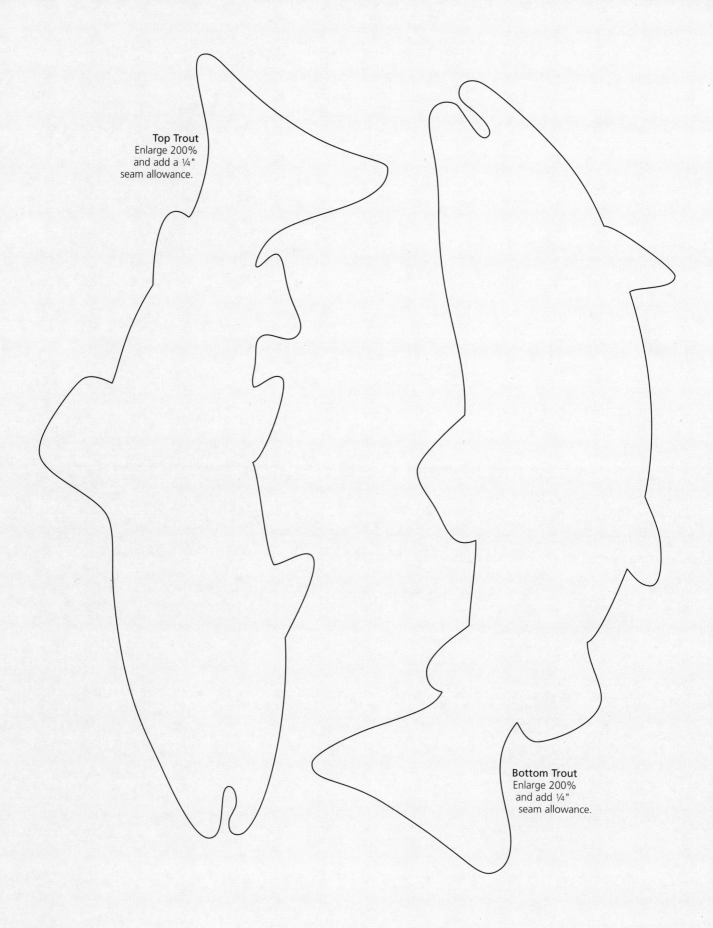

Top Trout
Enlarge 200%
and add a ¼"
seam allowance.

Bottom Trout
Enlarge 200%
and add ¼"
seam allowance.

midnight hoop dreams

Designed by Zack and Cyndy Rymer,

machine pieced and appliquéd by Cyndy Rymer,

machine quilted by Laura Lee Fritz

Quilt Size: 66½" x 90½"

While growing up, golf was the only sport my father watched on TV. Things are a little different in our household. With two teenage sons in the family, you have to make a lot of noise to be able to watch anything BUT basketball, football, and baseball. My son loves basketball, so we designed this quilt for his double bed. The arcing basketballs are every player's dream: each shot swooshes perfectly into the basket. Laura Lee Fritz did a great job with the machine quilting; there are players going up for a shot, basketball shoes, stars, and arrows.

Fabric Tips

Look for a range of values for the basketballs from bright orange to deep rust. The leftover darker rusts came in handy for the binding. Any tan would work for the background, but I felt fortunate to find the plank flooring fabric. You can customize the key (center of the court) for your quilt by making it in the colors of your guy's favorite basketball team.

After making yards of bias tape I discovered that you can buy pre-made black bias tape, which is definitely the way to go!

(Please note: This quilt was designed for a double-bed size platform bed, so the side borders would fit within the frame. You may want to add an inner border about 2" wide to make it fit a standard 54"-wide mattress, or make the outside border wider.)

Fabric Requirements

- Tan flooring fabric: 2¼ yards
- Blue for key: 1 yard
- Red for key: ½ yard
- Assorted oranges to rusts for basketballs, hoop, and binding: 2⅞ yards total
- Blue for borders: 2¼ yards
- Black ½"-wide single-fold bias tape: 3 four-yard packages OR ¾ yard black fabric
- Iron-on interfacing (used for the basketballs and upper part of key circle): 1¼ yards
- Iron-on tear-away stabilizer: 1 yard
- Steam-A-Seam® ¼"-wide tape
- White rayon thread for basketball hoop

Cutting Instructions

Flooring Fabric

Cut one rectangle 32½" x 39½".

Cut four 9½" strips, then piece end to end and cut two 74½" pieces.

Blue for Key

Cut one rectangle 32½" x 35½".

Red for Half-circle in Key

First make a half-circle paper template by folding a 32½" x 16¼" piece of paper in half. To form the half-circle arc, use a yardstick and pencil. Starting on the fold with the 16¼" mark at the center corner, slowly move the yardstick in an arc, making large dots at 3" intervals. Connect the dots to form the arc, and cut the paper template out. Place the unfolded paper template on the fabric and pin in place. Cut out the half-circle.

Interfacing for Key

Cut a half-circle from the interfacing that is about ¼" smaller than the red fabric half-circle arc.

Black Bias Binding Tape

If you choose to make the bias tape, piece together enough 1⅛"-wide bias strips to make approximately 11 yards.

Press strip in half lengthwise, then sew using a ⅛" seam allowance. Press so seam is in center of strip.

Basketballs

Have enlargements made of the basketball pattern on page 43 using the following percentages: 57%, 80%, 100% (same size as shown), 115%, 135%, 158%, 173%.

Choose two contrasting fabrics for each basketball. When cutting, add ¼" seam allowance for the internal seam allowances, and about ½" for the outside edges. Cut one basketball center from the darker of the two fabrics for each basketball using basketball center A.

Fold the fabric chosen for the basketball sides in half, and place Basketball side B on the right side of the fabric. Cut out the shape. You will have two side pieces.

Interfacing:
For each basketball cut a circle of interfacing.

Basketball Hoop

Cut a 3" x 38" bias strip of darker orange fabric.

Borders

Cut four 8½"-wide strips, then piece pairs together end to end and cut a 74½" strip from each pair for side borders.

Cut four 8½"-wide strips, then piece pairs together end to end and cut a 66½" strip from each pair for top and bottom borders.

Quilt Assembly

Key

1. Following the manufacturer's instructions, iron the interfacing to the wrong side of the upper half of the key (the red half-circle). Pin, then baste this to the top of the blue rectangle.

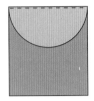

2. With right sides together, place the 32½" x 39½" upper flooring piece on top of the key, keeping the red upper circle folded down on top of the blue rectangle. Stitch the three layers together along the basting line. Press the circular part of the key up onto the upper flooring rectangle as shown.

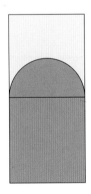

3. Sew the red upper key half-circle to the background using a narrow zigzag stitch.

4. Pin and then sew the 9½" x 74½" side flooring strips to the sides of the assembled court. Press seams toward the side pieces.

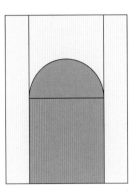

Adding the Black Bias Tape

1. Cut the following lengths from the black bias tape, but check the measurement on your top before you cut.

Small half-circle at top of quilt: 22½"
Arc above key: 57½"
Solid line at top of key: 51"
Dashed line: five 6½" pieces
Horizontal line through middle of key: 44"
Vertical side lines on key, and outside of key: four 35½" pieces

2. Back each piece of the bias tape with ¼"-wide Steam-a-Seam tape.

3. Remove the paper backing on the tape, and position each piece according to the diagram. When you are satisfied with the placement, iron the tape pieces in place. Sew to the quilt top using a narrow zigzag stitch.

Making the Basketballs

1. To piece the basketballs, match the registration marks, and pin the side pieces to the center section. Stitch. Clip the curved seams and press the seam toward the outside edge of the basketball.

2. Iron interfacing to the wrong side of each basketball. Clip curves of outer seam allowance, and press to back.

3. You're ready to add the decorative basketball seam lines. Back the basketball with the iron-on stabilizer. With black thread, add a ⅛"-wide satin stitch on all of the seam lines. Press basketball in half in both directions to create the additional lines to satin stitch. Remove the stabilizer.

4. Refer to the photo on page 39 and position the basketballs on the quilt top. Baste in place. Using a satin or blanket stitch, sew all but the largest basketball to the quilt top.

Basketball Hoop

1. With wrong sides together, fold the orange 3"-wide bias strip in half lengthwise. Sew using a ¼" seam. Press with seam centered in back. Pin to the quilt top. Follow the diagram for the hoop dimensions.

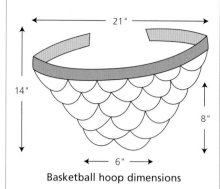

Basketball hoop dimensions

2. Position the ends of the bias tube behind the sides of the largest basketball. Sew the basketball and the hoop to the quilt top using a narrow zigzag or blanket stitch.

3. Using a chalk or silver marking pencil, freehand draw some guidelines for the net onto the quilt top. Iron stabilizer onto the back of the quilt top in the hoop area.

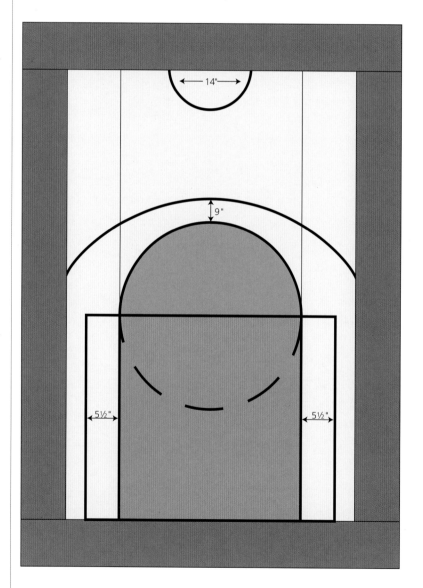

4. Using the white rayon thread and a wide satin stitch, stitch the net following your guidelines. Start stitching with a narrower satin stitch, gradually increasing the width of the stitch as you go. Decrease the width at the ends of each curve. Remove stabilizer.

Borders

1. Pin, then sew the side borders to the quilt top. Press.

2. Pin, then sew the top and bottom borders to the quilt top. Press.

Quilting

Photos from basketball magazines along with diagrams from basketball strategy books provided the inspiration for the quilting. Arrows, basketball shoes, stars, and basketball players taking a variety of shots were quilted throughout the top.

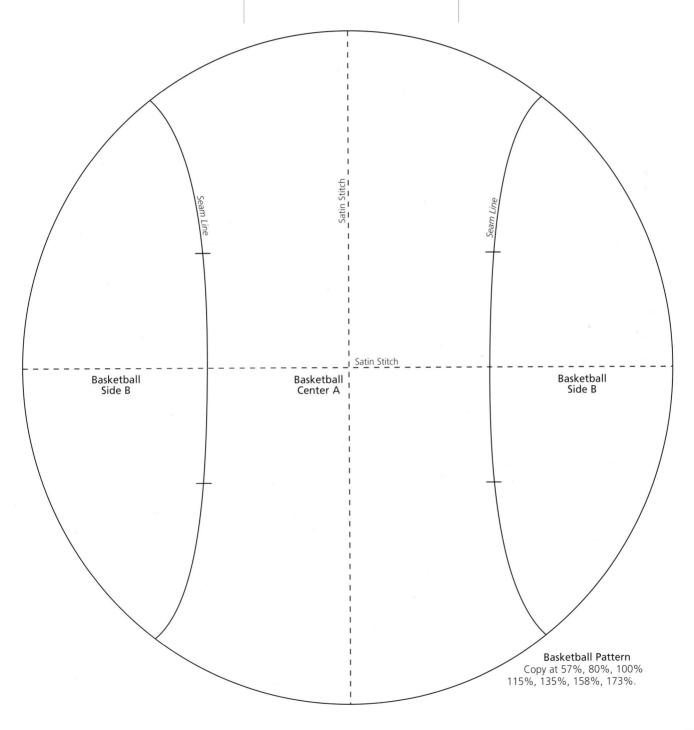

Seam Line

Satin Stitch

Seam Line

Satin Stitch

Basketball
Side B

Basketball
Center A

Basketball
Side B

Basketball Pattern
Copy at 57%, 80%, 100%
115%, 135%, 158%, 173%.

rainbow trout

Jean Wells, Sisters, OR

Quilt Size: 47½" square

When I was a little girl I used to catch rainbow trout in the Metolius River. Even then I was captivated by the colors I saw. When I discovered an antique quilt block that was shaped as a fish I drafted a pattern for the quilt. Paper piecing was the easiest way for me to complete the block. Rainbow-colored fabrics from the Fossil Fern Collection by Benartex were the right style of fabric for the fish. Clam shells and a continuous wave design were used for the quilting.

Fabric Requirements

- Black for the background, borders, and binding: 2 yards total
- Yellow, orange, red, melon, purple, blue-violet, blue, green: ¼ yard each
- Blue: ⅜ yard
- Green: ⅓ yard

Cutting Instructions

Black for Set 1 of Rainbow Strip Sets

Cut four strips 1½" x 22".
Cut four strips 1½" x 19".
Cut four strips 1½" x 15½".
Cut four strips 1½" x 11".
Cut two 5¼" squares, then cut in half diagonally.

Black for Set 2 of Rainbow Strip Sets

Cut four strips 1½" x 33".
Cut four strips 1½" x 30".
Cut four strips 1½" x 26".
Cut four strips 1½" x 22".
Cut two 11½" squares, then cut in half diagonally.

Fish Block

Cut two 6¼" black squares, cut in half diagonally for the corner sections. Scraps will be used for the rest of the piecing in the fish block.

Inner Border

Cut two 2"-wide black strips, then cut into two 18½" strips for the sides, and two 21½" strips for the top and bottom.

Outer Border

Cut five 3"-wide black strips, then piece strips together end to end using diagonal seams. Cut two 42½" strips for side borders and two 47½" strips for top and bottom borders.

Binding

Cut five 2¼"-wide black strips, then piece together end to end using diagonal seams.

Set 1 of Rainbow Strip Sets

Yellow:
Cut four strips 1" x 24".

Orange:
Cut four strips 1¼" x 20½".

Red:
Cut four strips 1½" x 17½".

Melon:
Cut four strips 1¾" x 13½".

The leftovers will be used to piece the fish.

Set 2 of Rainbow Strip Sets

Purple:
Cut four strips 1" x 31".

Blue-violet:
Cut four strips 1¼" x 28".

Blue:
Cut four strips 1½" x 24½".

Green:

Cut four strips 1¾" x 20".

The leftovers will be used to piece the fish.

Quilt Assembly

The fish block is divided into four sections made up of five units each. Piece one unit at a time and sew together to make a 9" square section.

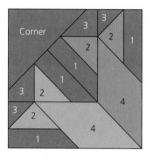

Refer to the color photograph for color placement. Enlarge patterns on page 47. Make four copies of each unit.

1. Begin with the tail and fish body Unit A and Unit A Reversed following the number sequence. See page 77 for instructions on paper piecing.

2. Complete tail Units B and B Reversed following the number sequence. Join to tail and fish body Unit A. Add the corner. Complete four sections and join to make the 18" block (18½" with seam allowance).

3. Add the side inner borders first, then the top and bottom inner borders.

4. To piece the first set of rainbow strips, mark the center of each of the strips and match up the pins. Stitch the strips together as shown below. Press the seams in one direction. Measure across the bottom of the strips 22¼". Trim at a 45° angle down each side. Add the corner triangle. It will be a little larger; trim it evenly.

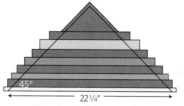

First Set Rainbow Strips

5. Repeat the same process for the second set of strips except this time start with a black strip. Measure across the bottom of the strips 31". Cut a 45° angle down each side and add the corner triangle. It will be a little larger; trim it evenly.

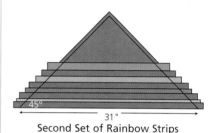

Second Set of Rainbow Strips

6. Add the final border, sides first, then top and bottom.

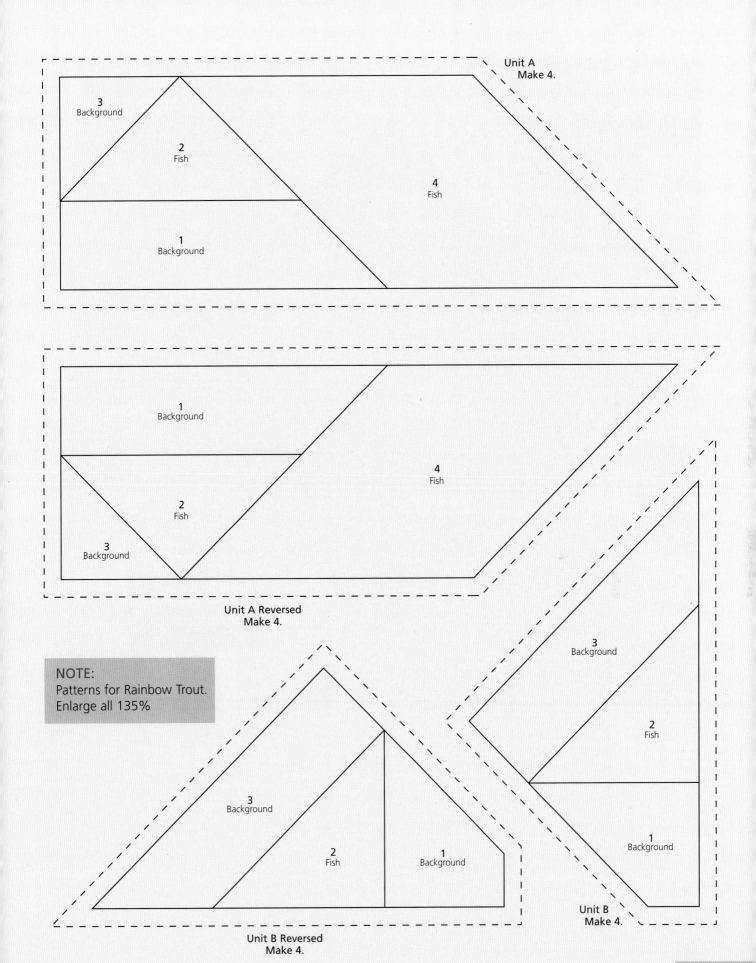

Unit A
Make 4.

3
Background

2
Fish

4
Fish

1
Background

1
Background

4
Fish

2
Fish

3
Background

Unit A Reversed
Make 4.

NOTE:
Patterns for Rainbow Trout.
Enlarge all 135%

3
Background

3
Background

2
Fish

2
Fish

1
Background

1
Background

Unit B
Make 4.

Unit B Reversed
Make 4.

recycled blues

Designed and made by the C&T Friday Quilters,

machine quilted by Judy Carlson

Quilt Size: 60½" square

Once the design for this quilt was drafted, an all-call for old jeans from C&T staff members yielded more than enough pairs to put together this quilt top during one afternoon sewing session. If you don't have enough old jeans to cut up, consider checking out thrift stores. The flannel we used was a combination of recycled shirts and flannel. And the flannel backing makes it a warm, wonderful quilt to cozy up with.

Fabric Requirements

- Six to seven pairs of adult size denim jeans in at least two shades of blue OR 2 yards total of assorted denims and two pairs of adult size jeans
- Assorted flannels for blocks and border: 1½ yards total
- Flannel for piping: ⅜ yard
- ³⁄₁₆" cording for piping: 4 yards
- Binding: ½ yard
- Backing: 3¾ yards
- Batting: 64" square

Cutting Instructions

Denim Jeans:
If you do not have large enough pieces from the jeans, randomly piece fabric and then cut the pieces below.

Light denim:
Cut four 12⅞" squares; cut each square in half diagonally OR enlarge the pattern on page 79. Place the short sides of triangle on the straight of grain, and cut eight triangles.

Dark denim:
Cut two 18¼" squares; cut each square diagonally twice to make eight quarter-square triangles OR use the same triangle pattern on page 79 for the light denim. Place the long edge of the triangle on the straight of grain, and use it to cut eight triangles.

Cut eight 6½" squares for blocks.

Pockets:
Cut two dark front side pockets and two light back pockets from the jeans; cut off seams and zippers, and square up to make the largest square possible from the pocket.

Assorted flannels:
Cut twelve 6½" squares for blocks and border.

Cut four 2"-wide strips, then piece end to end for piping. (We cut on the straight of grain but you can cut on the bias.)

(Cutting instructions for pieced border are on page 50.)

Quilt Assembly

1. Measure each pocket square to see how much you will need to add to make a 12½" square. To determine the width of the strips you need to add, divide the needed measurement in half and add 1". Cut denim strips that width and sew those strips to the four sides of the pocket square in the same way that you would a Log Cabin block (clockwise fashion). Sew on Strip 1, trim to fit, sew on Strip 2, and so on around the block. Press. Square up blocks to 12½". Make 4 blocks.

Add strips to all sides of pocket square as necessary to make a 12½" block.

2. Sew one 6½" flannel square to one 6½" denim square. Press. Sew pairs together to make four 12½" Four-Patch blocks. Press.

Make 4.

3. Stitch two pocket blocks to two Four-Patch blocks as shown. Press.

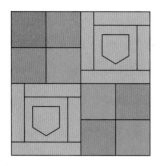

4. Stitch two dark denim triangles together as shown. Press.

5. Stitch large dark denim triangles to Four-Patch unit as shown. Press.

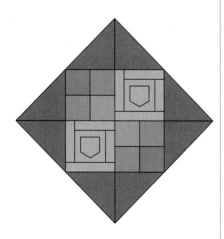

6. The 2"-wide flannel pieced strips need to be at least 150" long. Wrap around cording and stitch with a zipper foot as shown.

Trim seam allowance to ¼".

7. Use a zipper foot to baste the piping to all sides of the center unit.

8. To make corner units stitch light denim half-square triangles to two Four-Patch blocks and two pocket blocks as shown. Press.

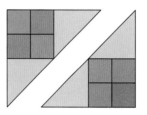

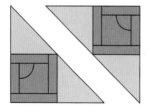

9. Stitch corner units to center unit using a zipper foot so you can stitch closely to the piping. Press.

Pieced Border

1. Cut assorted flannel and denim scraps into 6½"-wide strips of random lengths. Cut the strips into rectangles of random widths 1½" to 3½" wide.

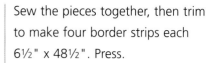

Sew the pieces together, then trim to make four border strips each 6½" x 48½". Press.

2. Sew two border strips to the sides of the quilt. Press.

3. Sew a 6½" flannel square to each end of the two remaining border strips and add to the top and bottom of the quilt. Press.

Quilting

Judy machine quilted in a random meandering pattern using YLI's Primary Variegated Jeans Stitch® thread, which added wonderful color to the quilt.

san francisco summer quilt

Pieced by Jeanne Neptune, Seattle, WA, 1999, and machine quilted

by Laura Lee Fritz, Middletown, CA; owned by Will Lapachet

Quilt Size: 58½" x 68½"

this quilt is based on the Chinese Coin pattern. I made it over a couple of years, changed presser feet in the middle, and didn't do much measuring. The only part of the quilt that was consistently measured is the basic "coin" rectangle. I mixed fabrics from my collection with fabric from my friend's collection (whose son owns the quilt) and with fabric scraps accumulated along the way.

This quilt provides you with an opportunity for improvisation. Once you have pieced the columns of rectangles, the rest is just a matter of adding on pieces and whacking them off to fit!

Fabric Tips

For the coins and pieced borders I suggest you collect about thirty to forty assorted plaid and print flannels. You need a variety of value and pattern scale in order to keep the combination of fabrics from becoming a static blur.

Fabric Requirements

Plaid/Printed Fabric

- Coins, Borders 2 and 3, and binding: 3 yards total
- Sashing and Border 1: 1⅝ yards
- Backing: 3½ yards
- Batting: 62" x 72"

Cutting Instructions

Coins

Cut fifteen 3½"-wide strips of various plaids. Cut the strips into rectangles 3½" x 6½" for a total of 90 coins.

Sashing Strips

Cut four 4"-wide strips lengthwise and trim each 54½" long.

Border 1

Cut four 4"-wide strips lengthwise and trim two 51½" long and two 54½" long.

Border 2

Cut 78 rectangles 3½" x 1½".

Border 3

Cut 40 rectangles 3" x 6½".

Quilt Assembly

1. Arrange the coin rectangles in five columns of eighteen coins each. Sew together. Press.

2. Sew the sashing strips between the columns of coins. Press.

3. Add Border 1 to the sides, and then to the top and bottom of the quilt. Press.

4. Sew Border 2 rectangles end to end into four strips: two strips with 18 rectangles, and two with 21 rectangles. Press.

5. Sew shorter Border 2 strips to the top and bottom of the quilt. Press. Trim to fit.

6. Sew longer Border 2 strips to the sides of the quilt. Press. Trim to fit.

7. Sew Border 3 rectangles together end to end into four strips: two strips with 9 rectangles and two with 11 rectangles. Press.

8. Sew shorter Border 3 strips to the top and bottom of the quilt. Press. Trim to fit.

9. Sew longer Border 3 strips to the sides of the quilt. Press. Trim to fit.

10. Measure the outside edges of your quilt and sew enough scraps together to make a 2¼"-wide strip for the binding.

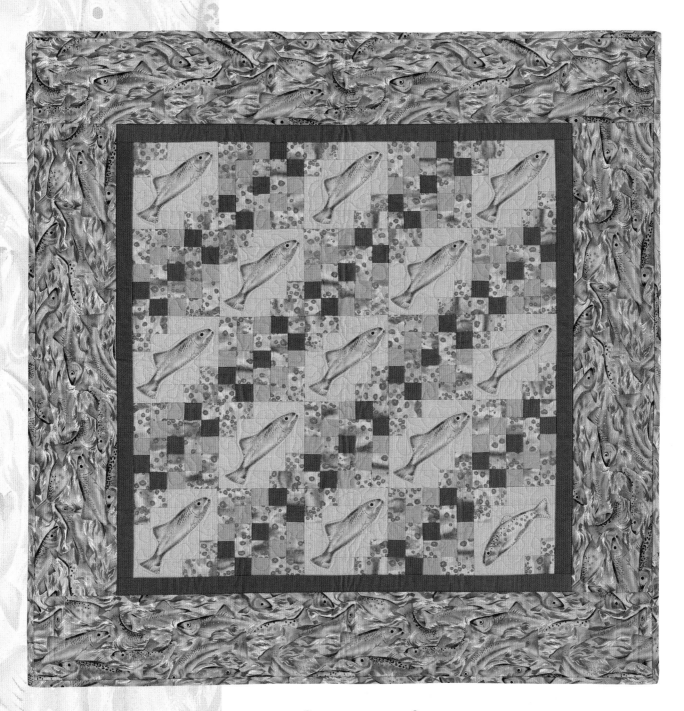

swimming upstream

Lucy Fazely, Oscada, MI

Quilt Size: 37" square

Finished Block Size: 5"

this small wall quilt was made as a market sample for Robert Kaufman Company. The charcoal and tan fabrics represent a rocky stream bed where the fish are swimming upstream to spawn. The fish in the bottom right corner reminds us that we can always go against the flow and be an individual.

Fabric Requirements

- Light gray solid: ½ yard
- Water print: ½ yard
- Tan solid: ¼ yard
- Dark gray solid: ⅜ yard
- Fish fabric I for appliquéd fish: 1¼ yards (or enough to fussy cut 13 fish)
- Fish fabric II for border/binding: 1 yard
- Backing: 1¼ yards
- Batting: 41" square
- Fusible web (12"-wide): 1 yard
- Tear-away stabilizer (22" wide): ⅔ yard

Cutting Instructions

Light Gray Solid:
Cut three 3½"-wide strips. Set aside one strip for strip piecing, and from other strips cut thirteen 3½" squares.

Cut one 2½"-wide strip.

Water Print:
Cut three 2½"-wide strips.

Cut four 1½"-wide strips.

Tan Solid:
Cut three 1½"-wide strips.

Dark Gray Solid:
Cut seven 1½"-wide strips.

Fish Fabric I
Cut thirteen fish for the appliqué blocks, leaving at least ¼" seam allowance around each.

Fish Fabric II:
Cut four 5¼"-wide strips for Outer Border.

Block Assembly

Block I: Make 13

1. Sew together a 2½"-wide strip of light gray solid with a 1½"-wide strip of water print and press. Cut twenty-six 1½"-wide units.

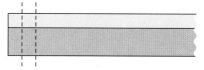

2. Sew together a 3½"-wide strip of light gray solid with a 2½"-wide strip of water fabric. Press. Cut twenty-six 1½"-wide units.

3. Sew a unit from Step 1 to the right and left side of a 3½" light gray square. Press.

4. Sew a unit from Step 2 to the top and bottom of each Step 3 unit as shown. Press.

Make 13.

5. Press the fusible web to the wrong side of the fish fabric for the blocks with the appliquéd fish. Cut out thirteen fish. Fuse fish to pieced blocks.

6. Pin a piece of tear-away stabilizer to the wrong side of each fish block. Machine button-hole stitch around each fish. Remove stabilizer.

Block II: Make 12

1. Sew together one 2½"-wide water strip, one 1½"-wide tan strip, one 1½"-wide dark gray strip, and one 1½"-wide water strip in the order shown and press. Cut into twenty-four 1½"-wide Unit A's.

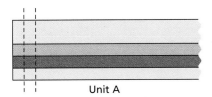

Unit A

2. Sew together one 1½"-wide water strip, one 1½"-wide tan strip, one 2½"-wide water strip, and one 1½"-wide dark gray strip in the order shown and press. Cut into twenty-four 1½"-wide Unit B's.

Unit B

3. Cut each of the following strips in half, forming 22" long strips: one 1½"-wide tan, one 1½"-wide water, and one 1½"-wide dark

gray strip. Sew together in this order: tan, water, dark gray, water, and tan. Press. Cut into twelve 1½"-wide Unit C's.

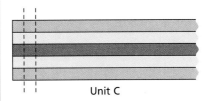

Unit C

4. Sew together Units A, B, C as shown. Press.

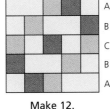

Make 12.

5. Lay out all blocks as shown. Stitch blocks into rows, then stitch rows together. Press.

Borders

Inner Border

Sew a 1½" x 25½" dark gray strip to the sides of the quilt top. Press. Sew a 1½" x 27½" dark gray strip to the top and bottom of the quilt top. Press.

Outer Fish Border

Sew 5¼" x 27½" strips to the sides of the quilt top. Press. Sew 5¼" x 37" strips to the top and bottom of the quilt top. Press.

The following companies provided materials used in making this quilt: Robert Kaufman Company, The Warm Company, and Coats & Clark.

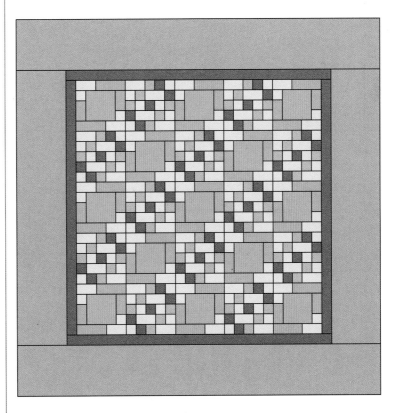

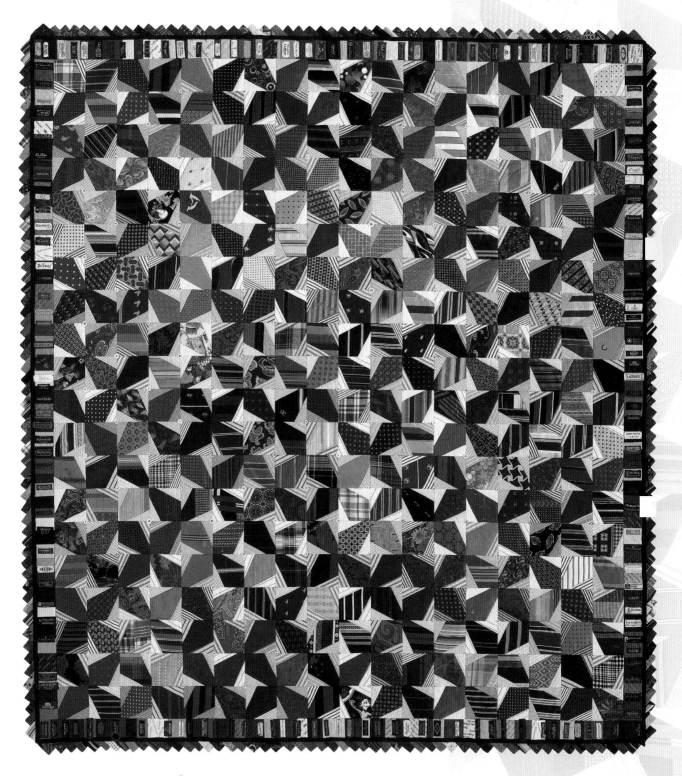

tie guy quilt

Wendy Hill, Sunriver, OR

Quilt Size: 81½" by 89½"

Finished Block Size: 8"

t *his scrappy quilt embodies*

the quilting spirit by using

recycled ties and shirts. You can

document decades of men's

fashions and tastes in a trea-

sured family quilt or a fund-

raising raffle or auction quilt.

Welcome all neckties because

even the ugliest looks great

in the mix!

All parts of the tie are used:

four ties make up a block; tie

linings make up the border; tie

labels embellish the border; and

tie-tails make "prairie points"

around the outside edge. The

pin-striped shirts accent the ties

and form "pinwheel stars"

where the blocks join together.

The shirt buttons punctuate

the middle of the stars.

Fabric/Supply Tips

Collect enough ties to make the desired size quilt. Any fiber content, color, and style of tie may be used, although extremely narrow ties may not be wide enough to cut out the kite shape piece. Next, assemble an assortment of oxford type, pin-striped shirts or shirting fabrics. Try to get a wide variety of colors and styles but avoid heavy or coarsely woven work shirts.

The ties make the quilt "dry clean only," so the search for the perfect backing can include rich, sleek "smoking jacket" type fabrics not typically used in quilts. (This isn't your typical quilt!)

If the quilt is to be hung on a wall select a batting that won't drape and buckle. Machine quilting is recommended because of the quilt's thickness.

The quilt is bound by bringing the backing fabric around to the front, with mitering at the corners. This simplifies the assembly process while avoiding the thickness of a double French-fold binding.

Fabric Requirements/ Supplies

King Size Quilt
10 by 12 blocks; 89½" x 105½" including prairie points
- 480 ties
- Shirting fabric: assorted pin-striped shirts and/or shirting fabric to equal 8½ yards
- Backing: 7½ yards (pieced crosswise); 9 yards (pieced lengthwise)
- Lightweight muslin (42"-45" wide) for foundation: 9 yards
- Lightweight fusible interfacing: 2½ yards (cut into twenty-four 3½"-wide strips)
- Batting: 90" x 106"
- 218 white shirt buttons (can use recycled buttons from shirts)

Queen Size Quilt
9 by 10 blocks; 81½" x 89½" including prairie points
- 360 ties
- Shirting fabric: assorted pin-striped shirts and/or shirting fabrics to equal 6⅓ yards
- Backing: 7 yards
- Lightweight muslin (42"-45" wide) for foundation: 7 yards
- Lightweight fusible interfacing: 2 yards (cut into twenty 3½"-wide strips)
- Batting: 82" x 90"
- 161 white shirt buttons (can use recycled buttons from shirts)

Twin Size Quilt

7 by 9 blocks; 65½" x 81½" including prairie points

- 252 ties
- Shirting fabric: assorted pin-striped shirts and/or shirting fabrics to equal 4½ yards
- Backing: 4⅔ yards
- Lightweight muslin (42"-45" wide) for foundation: 5 yards
- Lightweight fusible interfacing: 1⅞ yards (cut into eighteen 3½"-wide strips)
- Batting: 66" x 82"
- 110 white shirt buttons (can use recycled buttons from shirts)

Wall Quilt

5 by 5 blocks; 49½" square including prairie points

- 100 ties
- Shirting fabric: assorted pin-striped shirts and/or shirting fabrics to equal 1¾ yards
- Backing: 3 yards
- Lightweight muslin (42"-45" wide) for foundation: 2 yards
- Lightweight fusible interfacing: 1¼ yards (cut into twelve 3½"-wide strips)
- Batting: 50" square
- 40 white shirt buttons (can use recycled buttons from shirts)

Small Wall Quilt

3 by 4 blocks; 33½" by 41½" including prairie points

- 48 ties
- Shirting fabrics: assorted pin-striped shirts and/or shirting fabrics to equal 1 yard
- Backing: 1¼ yards
- Lightweight muslin (42"-45" wide) for foundation: 1¼ yards
- Lightweight fusible interfacing: ⅞ yard (cut into eight 3½"-wide strips)
- Batting: 34" x 42"
- 17 white shirt buttons

Other Supplies

- Iron-on transfer pen (Sulky brand recommended)
- Pressing cloth

Preparing the Ties

The ties need to be carefully taken apart and cut up. This takes more time than you might imagine!

1. Remove the tie label on the back of the big tie point (front), being careful not to make holes in the tie fabric. Save the labels.

2. Remove the stitching along the length of the tie. Discard the padding.

3. Remove the lining from the larger tie point (front). Save the linings.

4. Cut off the tie tails (the back point) about 4" from the point (or where the lining stops). Save the tie tails for the prairie point border.

5. Press all the component parts: the tie shapes, tie tails, and tie linings. Use a pressing cloth.

6. Cut the tie linings in rectangles 3⅝" wide by as long as possible.

Cut the fusible interfacing into 3½"-wide strips by the width of the interfacing (usually about 22"). Set aside.

7. Trace a paper cutting guide from the template on page 63. Place the guide at the bottom of the large tie point, paying attention to the placement of stripes, plaids, or individual motifs. Pin or hold in place and cut around the template with scissors or a rotary cutter. Remember, the cut shape does not have to be exact, just generously oversized for foundation piecing.

Preparing the Shirting Strips

1. Wash, dry, and press the shirts and shirting fabrics. Cut apart the shirts at the seams, discard the collars and cuffs, but set aside the buttons.

2. Cut the shirting fabric pieces into generous 2½"-wide strips, with the stripes running lengthwise. Cut the strips into generous 5" long pieces.

Preparing the Muslin Foundations

1. Wash, dry, and press the muslin. Cut 5"-wide strips and then cut the strips into 5" squares.

2. Trace or draw the unit pattern on page 63 onto heavy white or graph paper. Be sure this drawing is very accurate. A mistake here will be multiplied many times over

because this will be used as a "master block" to make all copies for foundation piecing.

3. Follow the manufacturer's instructions on the iron-on transfer pen. Using a grid ruler and the transfer pen, trace over all the lines of the unit, including the outside seam lines, onto paper. Center the inked "master unit" ink-side down onto a 5" muslin square. Hold in place while pressing the surface of the paper with a hot iron. With the paper still in place, lift up a corner to see if the ink has transferred to the fabric. If not, continue to press the paper until the lines have completely transferred. Repeat to make copies on the remaining muslin squares, re-inking the master unit as necessary.

TIPS:
- Press the pen lightly to avoid ink blobs.
- If you do get an ink blob, cover it up with tape, leaving the line exposed.
- Lift and place the iron; do not slide and glide or it will smear the ink.
- To get the most copies, iron for fewer seconds when the ink is fresh on the master unit; as the ink gets used up, iron longer and longer. You should be able to get at least a dozen copies from one inking.

Block Assembly

1. Assemble the units using basic foundation piecing methods. Place the tie piece right side down on the table. Place the muslin foundation square, lined side up, on top of the tie piece. Position it to your liking and pin in the middle.

2. Poke pins (through all the layers) in the "corners" of the first seam line. Flip the unit over. By visually connecting the two pins, you will see where the seam allowance is located. Choose a shirting rectangle, and place it right sides together with the tie, folding back the ⅜" seam allowance along one of the stripes. Align the fold with the pins, unfold, and pin the piece in place.

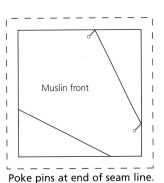

Muslin front

Poke pins at end of seam line.

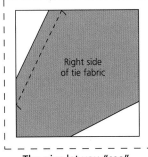

Right side of tie fabric

The pins let you "see" the seam line.

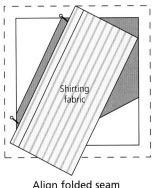

Shirting fabric

Align folded seam allowance with pins.

3. Flip over to the foundation side and sew along the inked seam line. Remove the pins, check placement, and trim the tie seam narrower than the striped fabric.

4. Press the striped fabric in place, using a pressing cloth.

5. Repeat Steps 2-4 with the remaining seam.

6. Make all the units required for the quilt size you chose.

7. Square up the units with a grid ruler to 4¾" square (the 4" finished size plus ⅜" seam allowance).

8. Finish the edges of each unit with a slightly narrow, open zigzag stitch. This will help when assembling the blocks and will strengthen the seams against raveling over time.

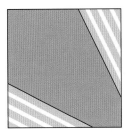

9. As you assemble the blocks, make sure there are four different striped fabrics in each block. Don't think about the color combinations too much; this is a scrap quilt, and just about any combination will look good.

To make the blocks, pair up the units and sew right sides together with a ⅜" seam allowance. Press the seams open to reduce bulk and make your quilt lie flat.

Pair up these half blocks to make a complete block as shown. Pin right sides together, matching the center seam lines. Sew with a ⅜" seam allowance. Press seams open. Repeat until all of the blocks are assembled.

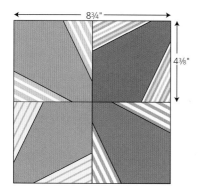

Borders

1. Sort the tie lining pieces into stacks by color (white, cream, black, light blue, red, yellow, purple, green, navy, etc.). Next sort each color pile into "solid" and "patterned." You will have two piles for each color.

2. With a 3½"-wide strip of fusible interfacing glue side up, select a variety of tie lining pieces to place on the strip. Vary the solids, patterns, and lengths of the pieces. Arrange them along the strip so the width of the tie lining piece (3⅝") covers the width of the strip (3½").

3. Make sure the raw edges of the tie-lining pieces are butted up against each other. Fuse the tie linings in place using a press cloth and following the manufacturer's instructions. Turn over and press from the back to make sure the pieces are securely fused. Repeat until you've fused all of the strips required for your size quilt.

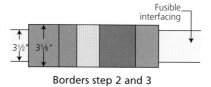

Borders step 2 and 3

4. Fold the strip right sides together where the raw edges of the lining pieces butt up against each other. Make sure the fold is at right angles to the long edges of the strip. Pin. Sew a ¼" seam allowance. Repeat to finish all the strips.

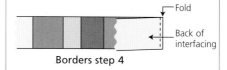

Borders step 4

5. Cut the folded seams open with sharp scissors. Press the seams open (this makes the border lie flat).

Quilt Assembly

1. Lay out the blocks on a design wall, orienting the blocks according to the photo. Notice that a pinwheel star forms where the blocks meet. Move blocks to distribute the brighter colors and to make sure that each pinwheel star has four different striped fabrics.

2. Assemble the blocks into rows. Press the seams open. Sew the rows together. Press the seams open.

3. Lay out the border strips along the sides of the quilt top. Move them around until you are satisfied with the placement. Sew the border strips together lengthwise with a ¼" seam to make four borders (top, bottom, two sides). Press seams open. Using a grid ruler, trim off both parallel long edges to make the border 3⅛" wide.

4. Pin the side borders to the quilt with right sides together. Sew with a ⅜" seam allowance. Press the seams open. Trim off excess border fabric at the top and bottom. Repeat with the top and bottom borders.

Quilting

1. Layer the backing (wrong side up), batting, and quilt top (right side up). Baste. Wrap the excess backing fabric over the batting and quilt top, turn under the raw edges, and baste to the border. This will keep the edges from fraying and the batting from pulling apart while you are quilting.

2. For the body of the quilt top, stitch in-the-ditch on the diagonal, following the seams between the tie and the striped fabric. Start with the two longest diagonals in each direction to anchor the layers. Continue quilting from the longest diagonals to the opposite corners in all directions. Use a monofilament for the top thread (such as Sulky polyester monofilament) and a thread color to match the backing for the bobbin thread. The stitching will go through the intersection of the ties in each block four times.

Quilting pattern

3. Stitch in-the-ditch in the seam between the quilt top and the border.

4. Unwrap the backing from the edge of the quilt border. Stitch in-the-ditch in all of the seams in the border.

Binding

1. Trim the excess batting without cutting through the backing fabric. Using a grid ruler, trim the excess backing fabric 1" from the edge of the quilt top and batting.

2. With the quilt right side up, fold the raw edge of the backing fabric to the edge of the border, then fold backing over the border to make a ⅜" binding that sits on the border. Pin as you go, mitering the corners.

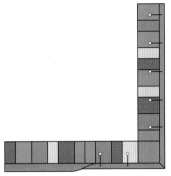

Fold backing to edge of border.
Fold again over edge of border
and miter corners.

3. With matching thread for both top and bobbin, topstitch along the edge of the binding through all of the layers, pivoting at the mitered corners. Hand sew the mitered corners in place if desired.

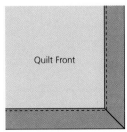

Topstitch along edge
through all layers.

Prairie Tie-Tail Points

1. To determine the number of tie tails needed for each side, count the number of units along the side. For example, if the quilt is ten blocks along the side, there would be twenty units. Allow two or three tie tails for each unit, depending how you want the prairie points to look. The quilt in the photograph has three tie tails for each unit.

2. Select the tie tails you will use. Using a grid ruler, cut the tie tails 2⅜" from the point to the cut edge. Line up the point and sides so the cut edge is parallel to the point.

NOTE:
Leave the little labels (if any) on the points; it is part of the charm of this quilt to note that a tie is silk from Italy or polyester from the United States.

3. Sort the tie tails into color piles (all bright reds, all dark reds, all light blues, all dark blues, etc.). Next, mix the colors/patterns into four piles so you have enough for each border.

4. Place the quilt on a flat surface wrong side up and with the right hand side of the quilt edge facing toward you. Begin placing the tie tails right side up, overlapping as you move toward the left side.

Without thinking too much, arrange the tie tails so that colors and patterns contrast each other, and the whole thing looks pleasing. Adjust the overlap so the points are more or less evenly spaced.

Pin each point to hold securely in place and baste along the bottom of the tails.

NOTE:
Unlike constructed prairie points, the tie tails are all different sizes so some will need to be overlapped more than others to distribute the points evenly.

Placing prairie tie-tail points

5. Thread the sewing machine with monofilament in the top and regular thread in the bobbin.

Turn the quilt over, and stitch in-the-ditch between the border and the binding. This will quilt the edge and stitch the tie tails in place at the same time.

6. Check to make sure there are no tucks or pleats in the tie tails. Trim the raw edges of the tie tails only to ¼".

7. Finger press the tie tails over the seam line and pin. They won't want to fold over willingly (because of the bulk of the seam), so press firmly. This time start at the left side and move to the right. Thread baste to hold firmly in place.

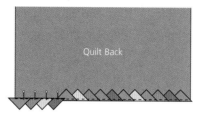
Finger press firmly and pin.

8. With thread that matches the binding/backing fabric for the top and bobbin, stitch from the top of the quilt along the outside edge of the binding, starting at one corner and stitching to the next. Pull the thread ends into the batting.

9. Repeat Steps 4-8 for the remaining four sides.

Finishing

1. Sew a white shirt button (by hand or machine) in the middle of each pinwheel star, going through all the layers.

2. Hand sew the tie labels around the border. Determine the top and bottom of the quilt and sew the labels on the vertical sides so they can be read. For the top, sew the labels from the right side to the left, and do the opposite for the bottom border.

3. Be sure to document the quilt by making a label for the back. Include the name of the quilt, the name(s) of the quiltmaker(s), the size, the date, the town and state and any other information, such as the occasion for making the quilt, and how the ties were gathered.

Patterns for Tie Guy Quilt

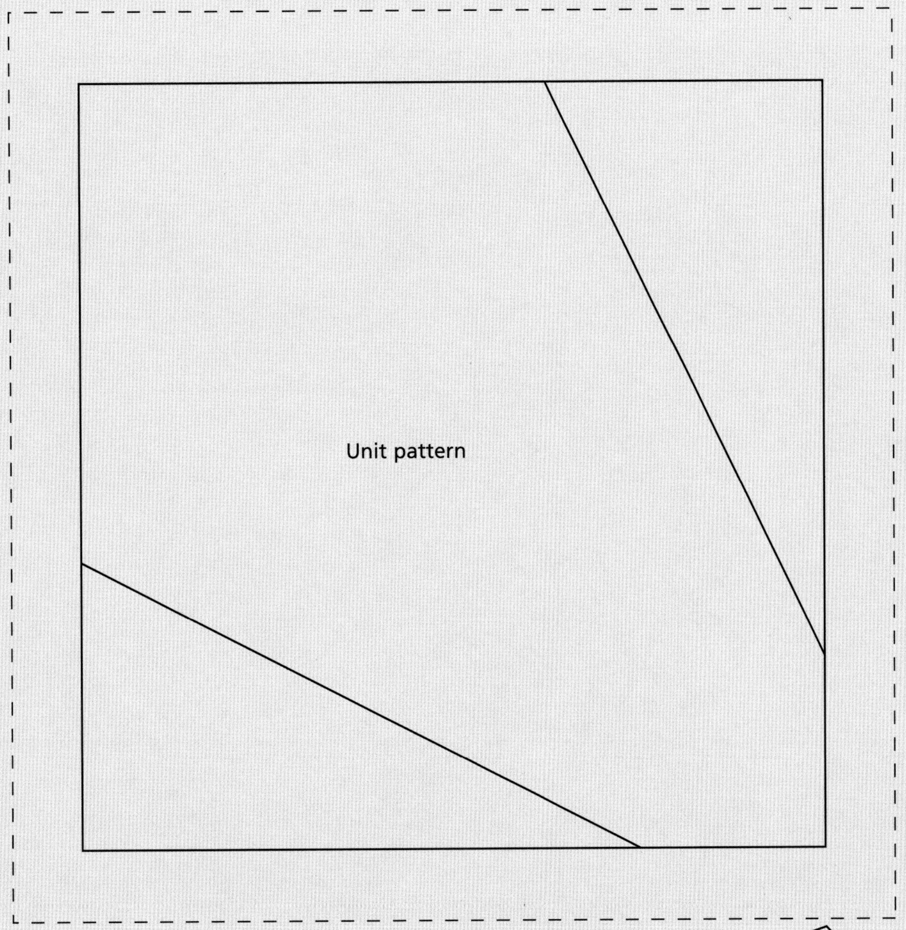

Unit pattern

Trace all lines with iron-on transfer pen.

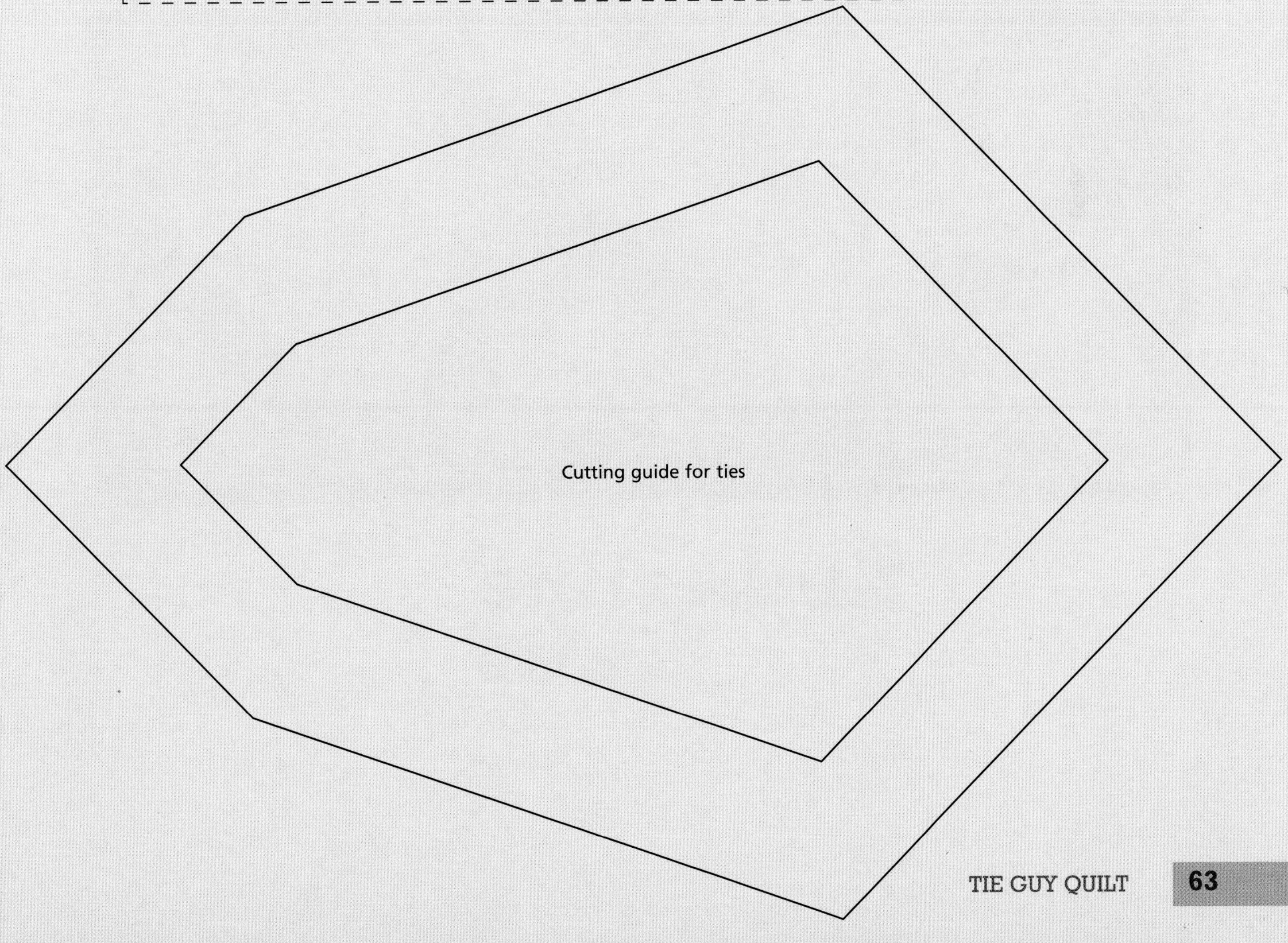

Cutting guide for ties

timberline trails

Janet Mednick, San Francisco, CA

Quilt Size: 79½" x 87½"

Finished Block Size: 8"

timberline Trails was designed during a family camping trip to Lassen National Park. It just "doodled" its way up while I was lounging lakeside one morning. Within a week of our return home I had completed a first version with 10" blocks in light and dark blues. (My teenage son was very impressed to see it jump off the graph paper and come to life so quickly, and as you know, it surely isn't easy to impress a teenager!)

I redrafted the block to 8" to increase the "trail" movement, and tried to recreate the high country color with every brown and beige fabric in my collection. I think of it as a "controlled scrap" quilt pattern.

Pick a colorway you love and cut into all of those fabrics you've been collecting. Another option is to go the totally scrappy route. Use whatever colors/fabrics you have, and just separate them into lights and darks.

Fabric Requirements

Quilt Body
- 14 dark fat quarters
- 14 light fat quarters OR
- Assorted darks and lights: 3½ yards each

Border
- Dark fabric: 1¼ yards
- Light fabric: ½ yard
- Binding: ⅝ yard medium-dark fabric
- Backing: 5¼ yards
- Batting: 83" x 91"

Total Pieces Required
- 90 4½" assorted dark squares
- 90 4½" assorted light squares
- 180 2½" assorted dark squares
- 180 2½" assorted light squares
- 360 2½" half-square triangle units

Cutting Instructions

You have two choices for purchasing and cutting the fabric for this project: you can use fat quarters, or buy yardage.

Using Fat Quarters

From each of the 24 fat quarters (12 light and 12 dark) cut:

Two lengthwise strips 4½" x 18", then cut into 4½" squares (8 squares total).

Two 2½" x 18" strips, then cut into 2½" squares (14 squares total).

Two 2⅞" x 18" strips. Set these aside.

NOTE:
These 2⅞"-wide strips will be used to create the half-square triangles. If you choose to use the grid system to make the half-square triangles (see page 12), it isn't necessary to cut these strips.

From two of the remaining fat quarters (1 light and 1 dark) cut:

Lengthwise into strips 2⅞" x 18". Set aside with other 2⅞" strips.

From the two remaining fat quarters (1 light and 1 dark) cut:

Lengthwise into two strips 2½" x 18" from both fat quarters. Cut these strips into 2½" squares of 14 light and 14 dark. (Set aside the extra fabric for emergencies.)

NOTE:
After all that cutting, you will have extra squares. Consider them to be insurance against cutting and/or sewing errors.

Using Yardage

From a total of 3½ yards of assorted darks and 3½ yards of assorted lights, cut the following strips:

Darks:

Twelve 4½"-wide strips, cut into ninety 4½" squares.

Twelve 2½"-wide strips, cut into 180 2½" squares.

Fourteen 2⅞" strips. Set aside.

Lights:

Twelve 4½"-wide strips, cut into ninety 4½" squares.

Twelve 2½"-wide strips, cut into 180 2½" squares.

Fourteen 2⅞" strips. Set aside.

Borders

Light Borders:

Cut nine 1½"-wide strips.

Dark Borders:

Cut nine 1½"-wide strips and nine 2"-wide strips.

Border Corners:

Cut one 1¼"-wide strip each from light and dark border fabrics.

Cut one 1½"-wide strip dark border fabric.

Block Assembly

1. Pair up one light and one dark 2⅞"-wide strip right sides together. Iron lightly so they "stick" together. Cut each pair into 2⅞" squares for a total of 180 pairs of squares.

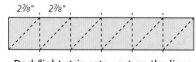

Dark/light strip sets—cut on the lines.

Cut each on the diagonal once, and sew each triangle pair together. (This is a good time to do some chain sewing.) Press open. You now have 360 half-square triangle units.

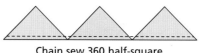

Chain sew 360 half-square triangle units.

2. Sew together two half-square triangle units, with one dark and one light 2½" square to make Unit C. Press. Make 180 units.

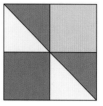

Unit C.
Make 180.

3. Sew together two Unit C's with two dark 4½" squares to make Block I. Press. Be sure the dark squares of Unit C point toward the center of the block. Make 45 blocks.

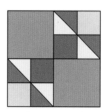

Block I (Dark)

4. Sew together two Unit C's with two light 4½" squares to make Block II. Press. Be sure the light squares of Unit C are turned toward the block center. Make 45 blocks.

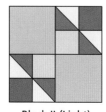

Block II (Light)

5. Lay out the blocks in your design area to match the quilt picture OR turn them this way and that, making your own pattern of trails and turns. Think of all the settings possible with traditional Log Cabin blocks. These simple blocks work in a similar fashion. There are endless variations to play with. When you are happy with your setting arrangement, carefully sew the blocks together into rows. Press. Sew the rows together. Press.

Border Assembly

1. Sew dark strips and light strips together end to end. Press. Sew these strips together to make the stripped border as shown. Press seams toward the center strip.

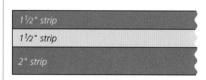

1½" strip
1½" strip
2" strip

2. Cut two border strip set pieces 80½" long for the side borders, and two border strip set pieces 72½" long for the top and bottom borders.

3. To make the angled corners sew a 1¼"-wide dark strip, a 1¼"-wide light strip, and the 1½"-wide dark strip together as shown. Press seams toward the outer strips.

1¼" strip
1¼" strip
1½" strip

4. Make a corner pattern template to cut four triangles for the corners as shown.

Cut four triangles with the 1½" strip at the bottom.

5. Attach the side border sets to the sides of the quilt top. Press. Sew corner triangles to each end of the top and bottom border sets as shown, being careful to match seams. Press. Attach borders to the top and bottom of the quilt top. Press.

Timberline Trails Top and Bottom Borders

Quilting

Timberline Trails was machine-quilted on a 25-year-old Kenmore. It was free-motion quilted without any marking. There are big free-hand feathers (brown rayon thread) running through the brown diagonal trails, and free-form leaves and swirls (beige cotton thread) quilted in the beige trails. A different "organic" shape is repeated in brown thread throughout the border.

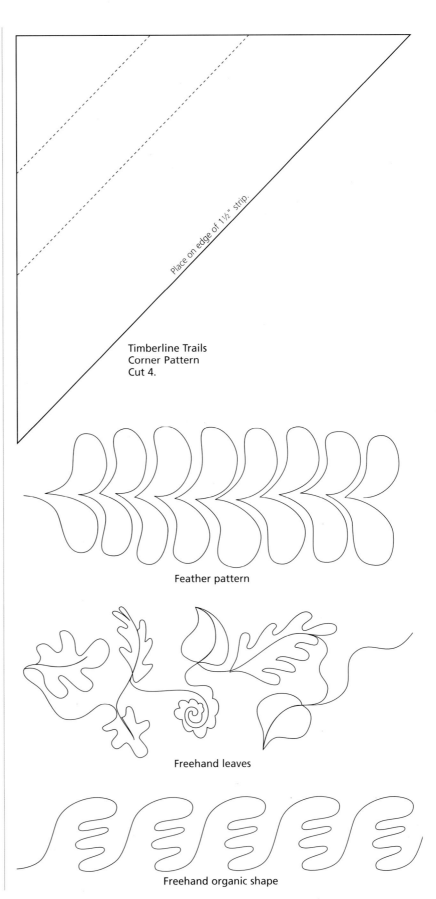

Place on edge of 1½" strip.

Timberline Trails
Corner Pattern
Cut 4.

Feather pattern

Freehand leaves

Freehand organic shape

What a Novel Idea

While looking for projects for this book an effort was made to find quilts that would appeal to a wide variety of guys. We realized that we couldn't possibly cover every hobby or interest that a guy might have. But what did happen is that we discovered those wonderful novelty fabrics, and there are a lot of them currently on the market. But as with potato chips or chocolate, it's hard to know when to stop.

We searched for blocks that offered large squares or rectangles that would show off that special piece of fabric. The blocks can be enlarged or otherwise altered if you choose a motif that doesn't fit within any of the blocks shown on the following pages. You can stretch the center rectangle as we did in the Unequal Nine-Patch block on page 69. Attic Windows, pictured on page 70, is another block that can be adapted to suit that great novelty fabric you found.

The novelty fabric doesn't have to take center stage; you can use it in the smaller areas of the block for a more subtle approach. See the golf version of the Stepping Stones block on page 70.

Making a sampler quilt with novelty fabrics is fun because you can make a block a day and never make the same block twice. By alternating the pieced blocks with plain blocks the quilt top could quickly grow from a wallhanging size to a wrap-around-him or bed-sized quilt. If the quilt were made in flannel novelty fabric, as the golf jams below were, it would be even cozier.

Finally, what can you do if you want to use even larger pieces of one novelty print? As you can see in the photo below, why not make him a pair of jams or boxer shorts? Use your favorite pattern, or see below for the patterns we used. The only tricky part may be finding the Sport Elastic, which was made with special sewing channels to make it easier to use.

While you may not be able to track down the same novelty prints shown here, there are plenty of new ones you can call your own. Happy hunting, and please send us photos of the quilts you make!

Cutting instructions are included for each 9" block.

Think beyond quilts when you want to make something for your guy. Patterns for the jams and boxer shorts pictured above are listed in Resources on page 78. Made by Joyce Lytle.

Boxer shorts pattern at left: Timber Lane Press (see page 78).

Jams Pattern in center and right: McCall's 2568, includes patterns for short jams, longer jams, and a pullover shirt.

Stretchrite® Sport Elastic manufactured by Rhode Island Textile Company, Pawtucket, RI 02862.

DOUBLE FOUR-PATCH

Two larger squares provide a great place to feature your novelty print.

A Two 5" squares
B Four 2¾" squares
C Four 2¾" squares

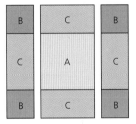

UNEQUAL NINE-PATCH

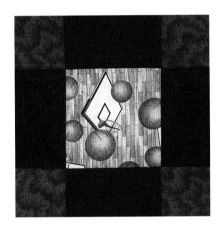

Love that large center square! You could use a coordinating fabric in the corners.

A One 5" square
B Four 2¾" squares
C Four 2¾" x 5" rectangles

UNEQUAL NINE-PATCH II

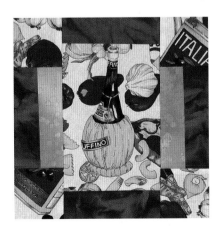

Here's a fun block to play with. The center rectangle can be shorter or longer; just adjust the size of the rectangles.

A One 7¼" x 5" rectangle
B Four 2¾" squares
C Two 1⅝" x 5" rectangles
D Four 1⅝" x 5" rectangles

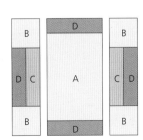

STEPPING STONES

Novelty prints work just as well on the sidelines. For smaller-scale prints, place the print in the B squares that form the diagonal "stepping stones."

A Four 2¾" x 5" rectangles
B Four 2¾" squares
C Four 2¾" squares

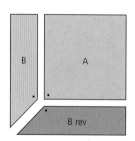

ATTIC WINDOWS

This traditional block can be adapted to showcase a variety of print scales.

Version 1: One 9" window
A One 7¼" square
B Use large pattern on page 79. Cut one and one reversed.

Version 2: Four 4½" windows
A Four 3⅞" squares
B Use small pattern on page 79. Cut four and four reversed.

SQUARE IN A SQUARE

An accommodating block, Square in a Square is wonderful for those larger-scale prints.

A One 6⅞" square
B Two 5⅜" squares cut in half diagonally

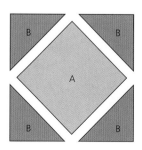

SQUARE IN A SQUARE VARIATION (ROLLING SQUARES)

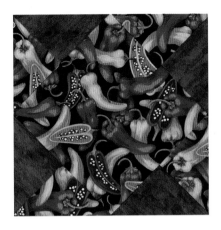

Love the way this block moves!

A One 6⅞" square

B One 5¾" square cut in half diagonally twice

C One 5¾" square cut in half diagonally twice

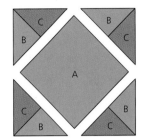

ART SQUARE

A more artistic rendering of Square in a Square.

A One 6⅞" square

B Four 2¾" squares

C Four 3⅛" squares cut in half diagonally

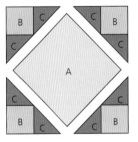

WHIRLIGIG (ALSO CALLED TURNSTILE)

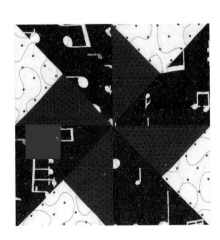

A new spin on an old favorite.

A Two 5⅜" squares cut in half diagonally

B One 5¾" square cut in half diagonally twice

C One 5¾" square cut in half diagonally twice

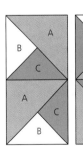

REFEREE

Referee is another block that offers a number of ways to use coordinating novelties.

A Two 5⅜" squares cut in half diagonally

B Four 2¾" squares

C Four 3⅛" squares cut in half diagonally twice

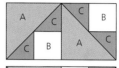

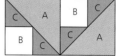

KING'S CROWN

A royal treatment for your favorites. So many possibilities!

A One 5" square

C Eight 2¾ squares

B Four 5" x 2¾" rectangles

D Four 2¾" squares

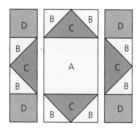

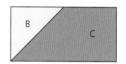

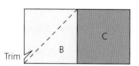

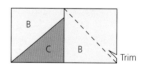

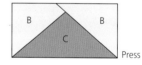

SAWTOOTH STAR

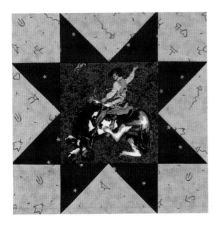

You can do the entire star in your favorite novelty print, or choose to follow our lead and use multiple fabrics. Just have fun!

A One 5" square
B Eight 2¾" squares (for star points)
C Four 5" x 2¾" rectangles (background)

D Four 2¾" squares (background)

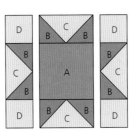

UNCLE VINNY'S FAVORITE

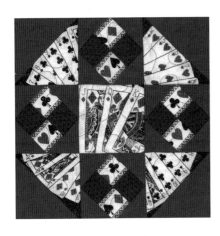

Aunt Vina taught Uncle Vinny how to make this block.

A One 3½" square
B Two 3⅞" squares cut in half diagonally
C Two 3⅞" squares cut in half diagonally
D Eight 1½" squares
E Eight 1½" squares

F Eight 2⅜" squares cut in half diagonally

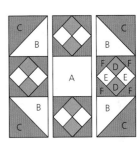

MONKEY WRENCH

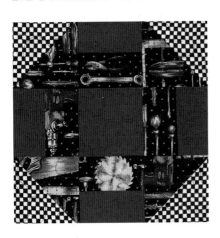

You don't have to use tools for this block, but we couldn't resist.

A One 3½" square
B Four 2" x 3½" rectangles
C Four 2" x 3½" rectangles
D Four 3⅞" squares
E Four 3⅞" squares

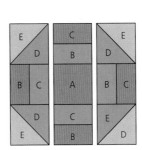

A few of his favorite things

Blocks and quilt top machine pieced by Carolyn Aune and
Cyndy Rymer, machine quilted by Judy Carlson.

Quilt Size: 39½" square

Finished Block Size: 9"

a sampler quilt with a "theme" was a must after making such a great variety of blocks. This was made with an imaginary guy friend in mind. He likes to go to Vegas occasionally (on his motorcycle, of course), enjoys a good meal, and smokes only an occasional cigar. He also enjoys tooling around with friends and listening to music. You can work out your own theme for your guy and substitute any of the blocks shown on the previous pages.

Fabric Requirements

Collect fat quarters of novelty fabrics before you begin this quilt, and you can fill in with tone-on-tones or solids from your stash.

- Blue sashing: ¼ yard
- Border 1: ¼ yard
- Border 2 and Backing: 1½ yards

Cutting for Sashing and Borders

Sashing

Four 2½"-wide strips, cut into six 2½" x 9½" strips for the sashing between the blocks, and two 2½" x 31½" strips for the sashing between rows.

Border 1

Cut two 1½" x 31½" strips for the side borders, and two 1½" x 33½" strips for the top and bottom borders.

Border 2

Cut four 3½" x 33½" strips.

Corner Half-Square Triangles

Cut two 3⅞" blue squares, then cut in half diagonally.

Cut two 3⅞" black squares, then cut in half diagonally.

Assembly Instructions

1. After making nine blocks of your choice, play with the block placement until you are pleased with the color balance. Sew the 2½" x 9½" sashing strips between blocks as shown in the photo. Press.

2. Sew the 2½" x 31½" sashing strips and block rows together. Press.

3. Sew the Border 1 strips to the sides, then to the top and bottom of the quilt top. Press.

4. Sew the Border 2 strips to the sides of the quilt top. Press. Make four half-square triangles with the blue and black triangles and add to the ends of the top and bottom border strips following the photo for placement. Add the top and bottom borders to the quilt top. Press.

Sewing Basics

Fabric requirements are based on a 42"-width; many fabrics shrink when washed, and widths vary by manufacturer. In cutting instructions, strips are generally cut on the crosswise grain.

General Guidelines

Seam Allowances

A ¼" seam allowance is used for most projects. It's a good idea to do a test seam before you begin sewing to check that your ¼" is accurate.

Pressing

In general, press seams toward the darker fabric. Press lightly in an up-and-down motion. Avoid using a very hot iron or over-ironing, which can distort shapes and blocks.

Borders

In most cases the side borders are sewn on first. When you have finished the quilt top, measure it through the center vertically. This will be the length to cut the side borders. Place pins at the centers of all four sides of the quilt top, as well as in the center of each side border strip. Pin the side borders to the quilt top first, matching the center pins. Using a ¼" seam allowance, sew the borders to the quilt top and press.

Measure horizontally across the center of the quilt top including the side borders. This will be the length to cut the top and bottom borders. Repeat pinning, sewing, and pressing.

Backing

Plan on making the backing a minimum of 2" larger than the quilt top on all sides. Prewash the fabric, and trim the selvages before you piece.

To economize, you can piece the back from any leftover fabrics or blocks in your collection.

Batting

The type of batting to use is a personal decision; consult your local quilt shop. Cut batting approximately 2" larger on all sides than your quilt top.

Layering

Spread the backing wrong side up and tape the edges down with masking tape. (If you are working on carpet you can use T-pins to secure the backing to the carpet.) Center the batting on top, smoothing out any folds. Place the quilt top right side up on top of the batting and backing, making sure it's centered.

Basting

If you plan to machine quilt, pin baste the quilt layers together with safety pins placed a minimum of 3"-4" apart. Begin basting in the center and move toward the edges first in vertical, then horizontal, rows.

If you plan to hand quilt, baste the layers together with thread using a long needle and light-colored thread. Knot one end of the thread. Using stitches approximately the length of the needle, begin in the center and move out toward the edges.

Quilting

Quilting, whether by hand or machine, enhances the pieced or appliqué design of the quilt. You may choose to quilt in-the-ditch, echo the pieced or appliqué motifs, use patterns from quilting design books and stencils, or do your own free-motion quilting. Suggested quilting patterns are included in some of the projects.

Binding

Trim excess batting and backing from the quilt. If you want a ¼" finished binding, cut the strips 2" wide and piece together with a diagonal seam to make a continuous binding strip.

Press the seams open, then press the entire strip in half lengthwise with wrong sides together. With raw edges even, pin the binding to the edge of the quilt a few inches away from the corner, and leave the first few inches of the binding unattached. Start sewing, using a ¼" seam allowance.